THE
RUSSIAN CONCEPT
OF WORK

THE
RUSSIAN CONCEPT
OF WORK

Suffering, Drama, and Tradition in
Pre- and Post-Revolutionary Russia

Anna Feldman Leibovich

Westport, Connecticut
London

HD
8526
L38
1995

Library of Congress Cataloging-in-Publication Data

Leibovich, Anna Feldman.
    The Russian concept of work : suffering, drama, and tradition in
pre- and post-revolutionary Russia / Anna Feldman Leibovich.
        p.   cm.
    Includes bibliographical references (p.   ) and index.
    ISBN 0–275–95135–9 (alk. paper)
    1. Work ethic—Russia.   2. Work ethic—Soviet Union.   3. Russians—
Attitudes.   I. Title.
    HD8526.L38   1995
    306.3'613'0947—dc20   95–3869

British Library Cataloguing in Publication Data is available.

Library of Congress Catalog Card Number: 95–3869
ISBN: 0–275–95135–9

First published in 1995

Praeger Publishers, 88 Post Road West, Westport, CT 06881
An imprint of Greenwood Publishing Group, Inc.

Printed in the United States of America

The paper used in this book complies with the
Permanent Paper Standard issued by the National
Information Standards Organization (Z39.48–1984).

10 9 8 7 6 5 4 3 2 1

Copyright Acknowledgments

The author and publisher gratefully acknowledge permission for use of the following material:

Excerpts from Vladimir I. Lenin, *Selected Works IX*, New York: International Publishers, 1937. Reprinted by permission of the publisher.

Excerpts from Boris Pilnyak, "Mahogany," in *A Bilingual Collection of Russian Short Stories*, introduced, translated, and edited by Maurice Friedberg and Robert A. Maguire. Copyright © 1965 by
Random House, Inc. Reprinted by permission of Random House, Inc.

Excerpts from Nikolai Berdiaev, "Philosophical Verity and Intelligentsia Truth." In *Signposts*, translated and edited by M. S. Schatz and J. E. Zimmerman. Irvine, CA: Charles Schlacks, Jr., 1986.

Excerpts from Nikolai Berdiaev, "Specters of the Russian Revolution." In *Out of the Depths: A Collection of Articles on the Russian Revolution*, translated and edited by W. F. Woehrlin. Irvine, CA:
Charles Schlacks, Jr., 1986.

Every reasonable effort has been made to trace the owners of copyright materials in this book, but in
some instances this has proven impossible. The author and publisher will be glad to receive information leading to more complete acknowledgments in subsequent printings of the book and in the
meantime extend their apologies for any omissions.

To My Family

When "leaps" and "breaks" occur in history, as in nature, they do not abolish the past. The sharper and stronger they are, the more clearly expressed is the return of life to the past, the restoration of an integral historical flux.

--V. V. Zenkovsky, *A History of Russian Philosophy*

I do not want history to enable me to escape the effect of the literary, but to deepen it by making it touch the effect of the real, a touch that would reciprocally deepen and complicate history.

--Stephen J. Greenblatt, *Learning to Curse*

Contents

Acknowledgments

This study has been done at the Department for International Education, New York University, New York.

I should mention with special gratitude Professors Philip Hosay, Donald Johnson, and Milan Fryscak, who were extremely helpful throughout. They followed this research from its beginning to its conclusion, and their discussions sharpened the focus of the study considerably. I am particularly grateful to Dr. Hosay, who was most helpful in editing the manuscript, for his thought-provoking questions and prodding remarks. My warmest thanks to Dr. Johnson for steering my research towards a "cultural" approach, and for his consistent encouragement. I offer my deepest gratitude to Dr. Fryscak for his gracious help and incisive observations, which guided me in my research.

My special debt is to my husband, Michael, and my two sons, Jacob and Joseph, whose stoic patience and moral support made a great deal of the work on this study not only enjoyable but possible.

Abbreviations

In citing works in Chapter 3, "The Function of Religion," and 6, "The Bolsheviks' Visions of Communist Work," short titles have generally been used. Works frequently cited are identified by the following abbreviations:

F: Stalin, J. "Foundations of Leninism." In *Stalin's Kampf,* edited by M. R. Werner. New York: Howell, Soskin and Co., 1940.

FD: Lenin, V. "From the Destruction of the Ancient Social System to the Creation of the New." In *Selected Works IX.* New York: International Publishers, 1937.

GB: Lenin, V. "A Great Beginning." In *Selected Works IX.* New York: International Publishers, 1937.

NEP: Lenin, V. "The New Economic Policy and the Tasks of the Political Education Department." In *Selected Works IX.* New York: International Publishers, 1937."

PV: Berdyayev, N. "Philosophical Verity and Intelligentsia Truth." In *Signposts*, translated and edited by M. S. Schatz and J. E. Zimmerman. Irvine, CA: Charles Schlacks, Jr., 1986.

S: Bukharin, N. "Speech at the Fifth Komsomol Congress, Oct. 11, 1922." In *Bolsheviks Visions: First Phase of the Cultural Revolu-*

tion in Soviet Russia. Ann Arbor Paperbacks: The University of Michigan Press, 1990.

SP: Stalin, J. "Speech at the First All-Union Conference of Managers of Soviet Industry, February 4,1931." In *Stalin's Kampf,* edited by M. R. Werner. New York: Howell, Soskin and Co., 1940.

SR: Berdyayev, N. "Specters of the Russian Revolution." In *Out of the Depths: A Collection of Articles on the Russian Revolution,* translated and edited by W. F. Woehrlin. Irvine, CA: Charles Schlacks, Jr., 1986.

Note on Translation and Transliteration

Unless otherwise indicated, all the translations from the Russian have been done by the author. For the transliteration of Russian words J. Thomas Shaw's *The Transliteration of Modern Russian for English-Language Publications* (Madison: University of Wisconsin Press, 1967), has been followed, using System II, except for those names with well-established English forms, such as Berdyayev, Dostoyevsky, Gorky, Tolstoy, and Trotsky.

Introduction

THE RUSSIAN AS THE SUBJECT OF STUDY: THE MARTYRED CHRIST

This book is an examination of Russian perceptions of work during the initial period of industrialization and modernization from the 1890s to the early 1930s, just before and after the Bolshevik revolution.

The recent collapse of the Soviet empire, the emergence of an independent Russian state, and the intense debate surrounding Russia's search for psychological, economic, and social stability in the chaos of the collapse reveal a gap in the existing body of Russian scholarship in the former Soviet Union, as well as in the West. For the most part, Russian studies of work have focused on either sociological (Leites 1985; Yanowitch 1985; Schlapentokh 1986) or economic (Berliner 1957; Nove 1986) considerations to the exclusion of cultural values. Although these studies provide valuable data on the structural deficiencies of the Russian economy and their detrimental effect on economic behavior, the studies ignore the individual and his perceptions of work.

Instead of treating the Russian as an object whose sense of work is conferred upon him by society, I have examined how the Russian "makes sense of work as his daily activity and brings meaning into it" (Joyce 1987, 5). The focus of this work is on Russian culture and its pervasive effect on socioeconomic and related political behavior. The study is confined to ethnic male Russians.[1]

I am concerned with the matters of symbolic representations and, particularly, with the representative symbols and anecdotes which crystallized the Russian's perceptions of work. My interest is, therefore, all-inclusive and encompasses religious beliefs, folk wisdom, and intellectual and literary wit.

In trying to grasp the Russian's conception of himself as a participant in social life between the 1890s and the 1930s, I searched out and analyzed "the symbolic forms--words, images, institutions, behaviors--in terms of which, in each place, people actually represented themselves to themselves and to one another" (Geertz 1983, 58). My findings led me to conclude that during the period under investigation, the symbol of the authentic Russian was an ambivalent figure of a sufferer and a martyred hero.[2] Behind the resignation of the sufferer is the zealot, with ardor for total cleansing, poised to bring the kingdom of heaven to the earth.

This ambivalent image was shaped and molded in the womb of a protracted history of servitude and tyranny. Crowded with illusions and phobias, the image endorsed the idea of work which oscillated between the resigned indolence of suffering and the combative heroism of self-sacrifice. The "otherworldliness" of Russian Christian orthodoxy in the context of the Western dichotomy of heaven and earth effectively split the Russian experience. The Russian Christian orthodox dualism celebrated the eternal life of heaven and declared earthly existence transitory and meaningless. Salvation and absolute good, the meaning of life and human activity, were attainable in the heavenly kingdom alone.[3] In Russian Orthodox Christianity, unlike Roman Catholicism, the idea of salvation is grounded in the concept of collectivity *(sobornost')* and, therefore, "not an individual person is saved, but the whole of mankind" (Berdyayev 1923, 125-26).

The Russian's perception of selfhood and the cultural webs sustaining the vitality of the image of sufferer and hero lie at the heart of the dilemma of work gripping Russian society today. The tendency of the image to celebrate the extreme and its susceptibility to controversy made possible an inquiry into the Russian psyche, the Russian's perception of man and his relationship with his physical and human environment.

Here I should introduce the terminology and method I shall employ. The notion of work in the context of this work refers to any kind of purposeful human activity, including the human activity that defines and shapes the quality of social life, gives meaning and purpose to social institutions, accepts or opposes political power, or perpetuates or undermines political, social, and economic policies. I have chosen to explore the Russian perceptions of work in the voices of the peasant suffering from the grueling experience of intense summer field work, the revolutionary calling for heroism and self-sacrifice, and the intellectual doubting the capacity for change. I have studied written and visual sources I would collectively refer to as works of art. I am not concerned with the discursive fields of literature or the visual arts; nor am I concerned with religion, folklore, and literary criticism. My interest is in the cultural history of work perceptions and how they manifest themselves in works of art, the objects of human creation.

It is assumed, following Stephen Greenblatt, that a "work of art is the product of a negotiation between a creator or a class of creators, equipped with a complex, communally shared repertoire of conventions, and the institutions and practices of society" (Greenblatt 1990, 158). When the Russian Christian orthodox image of the passion of Christ is made into the artistic representation of a heroic sufferer, the representative symbol negotiates the social practices and the author's perception of Christ as a "template for producing reality" (Geertz 1973, 95). For example, the image of the sufferer is accepted and celebrated as morally inspiring by the Russian Orthodox; however, it is censored by the Russian revolutionary, who emphasizes the humanism of Christ, his readiness to give his life to save mankind. The controversial, debilitating, and sublimating, effect of the image of the sufferer and the hero on the Russian conception of work has been the driving force behind this work.

When Russian society embarked on the course of industrialization, the Bolshevik leaders in charge of economic reforms recognized the vital need for a viable work ethic. A latecomer to industrialization, Russia seemed attracted to the Western model of industrial development and to Western conceptions of productive work.

Yet, however sound and appealing the Western model was, it was a product of a different socioeconomic and political structure, of a different culture, nurtured by different images and inspired by different illusions. The Russian revolutionary and religious intelligentsia *reinterpreted, absorbed, and accommodated* the Western conceptions of industrialization embodied in the Marxist-socialist visions of productive, society-oriented work and in the Protestant idea of the work ethic.

THE RUSSIAN VERSUS THE WESTERN CONCEPTION OF WORK

To better understand the cultural differences between the Russian and the Western conceptions of work, it is instructive to note first the similarities in the etymology of Russian and Western notions of labor.

In the Western European languages--Latin, English, Greek, French, German--*labor* denotes pain and effort;[4] the etymology of the Russian *trud* (labor) is the same. However, unlike the Western conceptions of work, which changed radically under the revolutionizing effect of the Protestant Reformation and the spread of capitalism in the West, the Russian counterpart remained anchored within the traditional system of values, which tended to view work as a life-sustaining, inescapable evil. Let us highlight briefly the cultural shift in the conceptions of work in the Protestant, capitalist West.

According to Hanna Arendt's study of the cultural evolution in the Western conceptions of work from ancient Greece to modernity, labor began the "sudden, spectacular rise from the lowest, most despised position to the highest rank, as the most esteemed of all human activities when John Locke discovered that labor is the source of all property" (Arendt 1959, 314). Following Locke, Adam Smith asserted that labor was the source of all wealth. The Western celebration of labor reached its climax in Karl Marx's theory of "labor productivity." In his enthusiasm for productive labor, Marx went so far as to suggest that "labor (and not God) created man and that labor (and not reason) distinguished man from other animals" (ibid., 76). Whereas labor for Locke was important so far as it served "the institution of private property as the root of society," for Smith labor denoted the perpetuation of "the unhampered process of limitless accumulation of wealth." But it was Marx who glamorized labor as "the supreme world-building capacity of man" (ibid., 8).

Yet, for all his glorification of productive labor, Marx was equivocal about the value of labor in modern society. He blamed the division of labor--when "each man has a particular, exclusive sphere of activity, which is forced upon him and from which he cannot escape" (Giddens 1971, 3)--as the primary source of man's loss of creativity. Marx visualized a future in which society would be liberated from the alienating effects of the division of labor. The new social system, in Marx's view, would give rise to new man, "the fully developed individual, fit for a variety of labors." This society of the future, Marx claimed, "makes it possible for one to do one thing today and another tomorrow, to hunt in the morning, to fish in the afternoon, rear cattle in the evening, criticize after dinner" (ibid.).

Marx's conception of creative work--unalienated labor--was heeded by Western European socialists as the prerequisite for a truly democratic social order. Socialism--the concentration of economic power and expropriation of the means of production for the common good--was seen by its proponents as the means of overcoming the alienating effect of the division of labor. Karl Kautsky, the executor of Marx's writings and the spokesman for the dominant trend in European social democracy before World War I, argued that socialist society, based on "collective ownership" of the means of production, would turn a worker into a "sharer in all the advantages of large industry; his conditions plainly bettered" (Kautsky 1976, 176). Kautsky held that under socialism "the competition which grinds down" would be eliminated and the "mainspring of economic development" would be "the power of attraction which the more highly developed forms of production exercise upon the less developed ones" (ibid.).

If Marxism and socialism looked upon labor relations and class struggle as the principal categories of social change, Max Weber identified religious beliefs, namely the "innerworldly asceticism" espoused by the Protestant Reformation, as the "innermost springs of the new capitalist mentality" (Arendt 1959, 228). Max Weber saw the link between the Calvinist concept of "calling" and the Protestant emphasis on mundane economic activities as moral duty to God (Giddens 1971, 127). The deepest motivations for mundane economic activities were worry and care about the self. Arendt argues that Weber's description of Western capitalist mentality as "world alienation" was far more precise than Marx's "self-alienation"(Arendt 1959, 230-31). Therefore, the most outstanding characteristic of the Westerner's conception of work, according to Arendt, is his belief in the power of human reason to "solve every issue." The holder of this conception believes that "every human motivation [can] be reduced to the principle of utility" and thinks of the whole of nature as "an immense fabric from which we can cut out whatever we want to [and] resow it however we like." He "equat[es] intelligence with ingenuity" and despises "all thought [which is] unrelated to the production of things" (ibid., 279).

Despite their ideological and methodological heterogeneity, the Western ideas of work--Marxist socialist and non-socialist alike--betray a common framework of cultural assumptions: belief in a common human history, in the power of human reason, and in the inevitability of progress; and the glorification of productive work as the source of social life.

Unlike this optimistic Westerner, the Russian at the turn of the twentieth century tended to view the concept of progress with deep suspicion and doubt. The Russian questioned the inhumanity of dispassionate reason, glorified the pain of suffering, and celebrated heroic deeds of self-sacrifice.

The persisting pattern of Russian cultural history, replete with failed revolutions[5] and abortive attempts at social change,[6] reveals a curious symbiosis between traditional Russian values and beliefs and the social structure. Russia's unsuccessful attempts at its own "reformation"--the failure of the Russian *raskol* (schism)[7] to become a vehicle of social change--demonstrate the tenacity of the traditional Russian value of resigned suffering, its Christian orthodox roots, and the cultural web of Russian religious tradition behind the Russian conceptions of work. Thus, the Russian's penchant to view labor as an inescapable evil--and a life-sustaining activity--represents almost a pastiche of the Christian conception of the sacredness of life. The conception, according to Arendt, "tended to view labor, work . . . as subject to the necessity of present life." Early Christians, Arendt persuasively argues, preached labor only "as a good means of staying out of trouble" (ibid.). Arendt finds the same attitude in Thomas Aquinas, who insisted that labor was "a duty for those who had no other means to keep alive" (ibid., 289-90). As for Jesus of Nazareth, "the only activity he recommends in his preaching is action" (ibid., 290), which is political: taking an initiative, leading the people. Arendt follows Weber in the belief that the change in the Western perception of labor stemmed from the shift of emphasis inaugurated by the Reformation, whose disciples claimed that personal, not universal salvation, "is the highest good of the man" (ibid., 291).

Seen from this perspective, the Russian *raskol* preached the value of personal salvation through good works, strove to shift the emphasis of salvation from the official Russian Orthodox church to the individual, within the context of Russian traditional values of suffering and self-sacrifice. Examination of the perceptions of work of the foremost supporter of the Russian schismatics--Lev Tolstoy--casts light on the peculiar Russian conception of personal salvation and on how it defined the Tolstoyan moral-philosophical conception of productive work. A closer look at Tolstoy's diaries makes especially poignant the process of intellectual accommodation between the new and the traditional conceptions of work. Tolstoy, faithful to the traditional Russian value of the passion of Christ, endowed it with the Western ethic of self-improvement.

The same tendency for appropriation and accommodation of Western conceptions within the context of the Russian intellectual's traditional conception of work as a heroic deed of self-sacrifice has been at work at the Russian revolutionary's reinterpretation of Marxism-socialism. Inasmuch as Marxist-socialist conceptions of egalitarian society, socialized means of production, and popular participation in production control were in harmony with the Russian traditional values of universal salvation, the Russian revolutionary embraced them without qualifications. However, Marxist-socialist insistence on the capitalist stage of production as an obligatory precursor of socialist social organization was rejected by Bolsheviks. Lenin's justification of an "historical leap" from an agrarian to a socialist society gave voice to his traditional aversion to the Western, Marxist value of work--a blend of rationalized search for profit and ruthless exploitation. Although Marx and socialists, despite their criticism of the rapacious capitalist work ethic, gave it credit for its contribution to Western progress, Lenin and other Bolshevik leaders adapted Marxism within the Russian context of self-sacrifice and universal salvation. It has been historians' neglect of Russian culture that has led them to attribute Lenin's opposition to economic struggle to his political ambitions alone. The findings of this research bring into the picture a very important missing component--the cultural, Russian Christian orthodox censorship of profit and money-making activities. While the ethic of self-sacrifice was conducive to political struggle and martyrdom, it was averse to the economic ends, that were intrinsically linked to the work ethic: rationalization and calculation directed towards economic success.

It is an historic irony that the Bolshevik leaders found themselves hostages of the native image of the heroic martyr. Unable to disengage themselves from the cultural webs of the significance of the ethnic meaning of work, Russian Bolshevik leaders set out to recreate a new socialist order within the traditional set of conceptions. Lenin's despairing complaint that "communists are [not leading,] rather they are being led" meant that Communist ideology and its Western conception of work has been renegotiated and restructured in the course of the postrevolutionary reconstruction.

The fact that there still is no adequate term in the Russian language for *work ethic* underscores the persistence of the traditional Russian perception of work. Instead of the notion of work ethic, the Russian language has a more narrow utilitarian term: "labor discipline." Stalin's industrialization drive, launched in 1928, and the "first five year plan frenzy (1928-1932)" (Lewin 1985, 222) represent a continuous and a losing battle by the party leadership to enforce labor discipline by the most brutal measures. For example, "a law of November 15, 1932, prescribed dismissal, denial of food rations, denial of access to food shops, and eviction from lodgings regardless of the time year." To raise the productivity of labor, the party leadership enforced piecework, the spreading of the pay differential, the promotion and offer of better food and priority in lodging, vacations, and school admissions to outstanding workers and their children and to those who stayed long enough on the job (ibid.).

The brutal excesses of Stalin's industrialization and modernization drive beginning in 1928 serve as an implicit recognition by the Soviet leadership that the Marxist conception of work remained a part of the Soviet work myth rather than sociocultural reality. The Bolshevik visionaries, acutely aware of the pain of labor and seeking to transcend it in the pathos of the heroic deed of self-sacrifice, renegotiated and absorbed the Marxist ideas of communist society within the framework of the traditional Russian conceptions of work. The contemporary collapse of the socioeconomic structure has revealed that the assumption about the possibility of imposing the work ethic is not sound.

To conclude, comparison of the Russian conception of work with its Western counterpart reveals that despite the similarities in the etymological origins of labor, their historical paths diverged. Whereas Western conceptions elevated labor from the demeaning status of activity associated with pain and effort to a glorious position associated with property, wealth, and personal ambition, the Russian traditional conception of work as resigned suffering, the heroic deed, and self-sacrifice remained unchanged. For the Russian peasant, work signified suffering and pain and prompted him to search for alternative routes in manipulation and trickery to alleviate his distress. For the educated Russian, removed from the immediacy of the peasant's painful experience, work signified either resignation to the existing reality or a violent attempt to eradicate it. The Russian revolutionary intelligentsia accepted Marxism with qualifications, within the context of traditional conceptions of work in Russia. They selectively appropriated Marx's theory of class conflict and revolutionary struggle, as well as his invectives against the exploitative nature of capitalist work, which gave legitimacy to the revolutionaries' celebration of the heroic revolutionary deed of self-sacrifice and universal salvation. But Marx's celebration of the creative powers of capitalist labor, alien to the Russian cultural paradigm of work values, remained muted. Marx's conceptions of labor, communist work in particular, were resurrected in the Bolshevik ideology of labor as the means of giving legitimacy to the Bolsheviks' industrialization and modernization drive. The hostages of traditional cultural values of work, the Bolshevik visionaries appealed to the Marxist vision of communism to accommodate their urgent need for the intense human effort of heroism and self-sacrifice.

THE RUSSIAN PERCEPTIONS OF WORK AS A CHALLENGE TO THE WESTERN THEORIES OF DEVELOPMENT

The remarkable persistence and endurance of the Russian perceptions of work between 1890 and 1935, despite fundamental changes in the political and socioeconomic structure of Russian society, challenges the ideological assumptions and theoretical presumptions of development theories. The findings of this research reveal a basic flaw in the current discourse on development--the neglect of the human agent and his perceptions of the contemporary socioeconomic and political reality. Even though the discourse on development is highly diverse and fluid, the modes of interpretation of social change have tended to assign to the individual a passive role as an object of change. In my critique of theories of development, I will deal separately with each school of thought, which, for the purpose of this work, I identify as modernization, dependency/neo-Marxist, and world-system theories.

The persistence and resilience of the Russian's perception of work question the assumptions about the universal character and homogenizing effects of social change espoused by the modernization school and rooted in early nineteenth century evolutionary and mid-twentieth century Parsonian structural-functional theories. Within the context of evolutionary theory, social change has been regarded as unidirectional, progressive, and gradual, rather than revolutionary, abrupt, and violent. Following this line of discourse, Walt Rostow, Neil Smelser, and Marion Levy spoke about a common pattern of modernization, distinguished by different stages of development. "The patterns of modernization are such," observed Levy, "that the more highly modernized societies become, the more they resemble each other" (So 1990, 33).

Schooled in the functionalist theory of Talcott Parsons, the proponents of modernization theory adopted the Parsonian concept of "pattern-variables" as a universal paradigm of social relations embedded in the cultural system (So 1990, 21). According to the Parsonian model, social change is a search for equilibrium and harmony whereby the institutions that constitute the system are always changing and adjusting. The modernization theoreticians emphasized ideology as a decisive factor in changing "traditional" societal values to "modern." "Values of ascetic and this-worldly religious beliefs, xenophobic national aspirations, and political ideologies such as socialism," Smelser asserted, "provide a 'lever' 'to pry' individuals from 'the attachments' to 'established commitments'"(Smelser 1967, 265). The modernization theorists, therefore, assume that individual perceptions and the particularities of societal values are prone to "social engineering" under the influence of ideology. For, as Parsons wrote, "the requisite system of values (associated with the capitalist mode of production) need not arise spontaneously within the society." It may be "institutionalized through processes which are analogous to the internalization of adult culture by children--namely, by what anthropologists would call 'diffusion'" (Parsons 1960, 19).

The underlying perception that social histories differ only in the stages of development led Smelser to cast off national histories and to conclude that socialism and capitalism are on the road to convergence. Thus Smelser's unbounded optimism in the self-sustained dynamics of modernization in the social structure led him to conclude that the Soviet Union "seems to be introducing more 'independent'[8] market mechanisms and 'freer' social scientific investigation in some spheres" (Smelser 1967, 265).

Following the same line of discourse that values can be imposed, the David McClelland study on achievement motivation (McClelland 1964, 165-78) suggests that the value of achievement can be taught as part of socialization in the course of modernization. The premise of the study is that there is a strong correlation between achievement motivation and economic development.

The persistence and resilience of the Russian traditional perceptions of work suggest several fallacies in the modernization theory. First, the dichotomy between traditional and modern has proved to be unfeasible. Second, the Soviet ideology failed to socialize people in "modern" values of work. Third, the assumption that modernizing societies exhibit the same pattern of development neglects the cultural peculiarities of Russia, which industrialized and modernized without the democratic changes that accompanied the Western process of modernization.

Although the neo-Marxist or dependency school has been critical of modernization theorists, it shares with them the analytical framework of the general process of development. Within this analytical framework, man as the subject of social change and cultural particularism has been as neglected as in the modernization theories. Unlike the modernization school, however, the dependency school's conceptual framework has been defined by the Third World perspective, premised on the assumption that dependency is the result of external pressures. Within this conceptual framework, dependency--distortion in economic production caused by the imposition of colonial dominance, which persists after the country has achieved independence--becomes the concept key in explaining social change.[9]

The dependency school has been rooted in the theoretical assumptions of "ELCA (UN Economic Commission for Latin America) and radical neo-Marxism" (So 1990, 107). ELCA assumed that the end of underdevelopment could be brought about by economic independence from the developed countries and rapid industrialization. The latter, it was assumed, would automatically bring social change. Another theoretical heritage of dependency theory has been neo-Marxism, which denied the classical Marxist belief in the capitalist stage of development. Neo-

Marxists premise their theory on the assumption that the Third World can skip the capitalist stage and build a socialist society. Unlike classical Marxists, neo-Marxists see the peasantry as the revolutionary force of change. Based on these theoretical assumptions, Andre Gunder Frank developed a "metropolis-satellite" model to explain how external relations have affected and defined all levels of social life in Third World countries (ibid., 97). "A mounting body of evidence suggests," Frank wrote, that the capitalist system has had a pervasive effect on "the economic, political and cultural institutions and relations" (Frank 1988, 110-111).

Another exponent of the dependency theory, Samir Amin, challenges the Marxist and modernization schools' assumptions that there is a universal pattern of capitalist development in the center and periphery. He brings in vast historical data to support his premise that the paths of development in Africa and European countries were different. Amin's theory is premised on an assumption similar to Frank's that "the capitalist mode of production constitutes a world-system." The "formations, central and peripheral" within this system, Amin suggests, "are arranged in a single system, organized and hierarchical" (Amin, in Ruccio and Simon 1988, 158). Amin points to the "hierarchical" relationships between center and periphery as the decisive factor in the underdevelopment of Third World countries.

This work on the Russian perceptions of work, however, reveals that the dependency school's assumption that the capitalist system has been the dominant variable in cultural institutions and relations is untenable. The dependency theory, which has reduced a complex process of social change to a single denominator--economic dependency--fails to account for the absence of "automatic change" in the Russian perceptions of work in the course of modernization. The findings of this study demonstrate that economic change in the course of modernization is negotiated and accommodated within the cultural system of beliefs. Neglect of culture as a variable in the model makes the model abstract and not applicable for a specific policy decision-making process.

The world-system approach, as discussed above, suffers from the neglect of man as the subject of study and does not take into account cultural peculiarities. The world-system--the key concept of analysis-- directs research away from the realm of the particular into the realm of the global. According to Alvin So, the emergence of the world-system perspective has been a reaction to "the economic stagnation in the socialist states, and gradual opening of the socialist states to capitalist investment" (So 1990, 170). So traces the theoretical heritage of the world-system perspective to the neo-Marxist literature of development and to the French Annales school (ibid., 171). The neo-Marxist conceptions have been explained in the above discussion. The French Annales advance Fernand Braudel's argument that history has to be studied as a total, global entity. The leading proponent of the world-system theory, Immanuel Wallerstein, accepts the dependency school assumption that the people in the colonies (he refers to his experience in Africa during the colonial era) tend to view "the reality in which they lived as a 'colonial situation,'" one determined by "the constraints of a single legal and social entity" (Wallerstein 1974, 4). Wallerstein rejects the notion of "stages of development" and proposes "the world context of any given era" as a variable, which effectively eradicates the notion of stages as incompatible with the notion of given era (ibid.,6). Social change then, Wallerstein asserts, could be studied only in social systems (ibid.,7). Wallerstein outlines his model as a description of the "world-system at a certain level of abstraction, . . . the evolution of structures of the whole system" (ibid.,8). Wallerstein's focus on the capitalist world economy reduces the study of social change to what So aptly calls "trimodal theoretical structure: core-semiperiphery-periphery" (So 1990, 195). Within the context of the world-system, Russia's course of modernization is seen as the interplay of external forces, whose dynamics fail to explain the particularities of Russian course of modernization and industrialization and which, as the findings of this study demonstrate, were defined and shaped by cultural particularism rather than by the forces outlined in the world-system model.

Against the deficiencies of the three models discussed above, I find the anthropological approach to the study of social change in the newly modernizing societies particularly useful. Clifford Geertz proposes a theory of social change whereby cultural and social aspects of life are introduced as "independently variable, yet mutually dependent factors" (Geertz 1973, 144). Geertz suggests that in societies that have been stable over an extended period of time there would be a "close adjustment between social and cultural aspects," whereby in most societies where change is a regular factor, there will be "radical discontinuities between the two." In those discontinuities, Geertz argues, can be found "some of the primary forces of change" (ibid.). Geertz distinguishes culture and social system as two different analytical frameworks. The cultural framework represents "an ordered system of meaning and symbols, in terms of which social interaction takes place." This framework includes "beliefs, expressive symbols and values in terms of which individuals define their world, express their feelings." The social system, Geertz says, is "the pattern of social interaction itself" (ibid., 144-45). Geertz sees "the nature" of the distinction between culture and social system in the "contrasting sorts of integration characteristic of each other." Geertz points out the differences in the forms of integration--"logico-meaningful" characteristic of culture and "causal-functional" characteristic of social system--as the cause of tension between them and personality structure (ibid., 145).

The findings of the present book, which point to the persistent discontinuities between the Russian's perceptions of work and his social structure, support the Geertzian conceptual framework of logico-meaningful and causal-functional integration. Within this conceptual framework, what occurred between 1890 and 1935 was not so much a destruction of traditional Russian way of life as a construction of a new one, a search, in Geertz's apt expression, "for the new, more generalized, and flexible patterns of beliefs and value" (ibid., 150). It is within this complex conception of the relations between religious belief and secular social life that we can deal adequately with the process of transformations from the image of suffering Christ to the image of suffering peasant, from Christian martyr to communist martyr.

This religious image of the passion of Christ and its underlying conceptions--suffering, self-sacrifice, and salvation--have constituted the paradigm of the Russian meanings of work. It was the image that shaped and molded the Russian Marxist's sociopolitical thought. For, Geertz insists, sociopolitical thought--ideology--is an integral part of "meaning" in "social and psychological contexts" (ibid., 196). The configuration of such dissimilar meanings of work in the Bolshevik's visions of communist work as Russian self-sacrifice and salvation and Western rationality and efficiency demonstrates the complex semantic structure of the ideological symbol conferred by the interplay between the semantic structure and the social reality of modernizing Russia. The key to the persistence and resilience of the Russian traditional conception of work is offered in Geertz's conceptualization of tensions between "local traditions--which are . . . essentialist" and "the general movement of contemporary history--that is, epochalist" (ibid., 243). Looked upon within this framework of tensions, the Bolshevik's vision of communist work represented an attempt to "cast an epochalist hope," or moderniza-tion drive, into "specific symbolic form," which would combine the Russian and the Western conceptions of work and perpetuate the process of "collective self-redefinition" (ibid., 252).

Thus, unlike the Parsonian modernization model, which suggested a preexisting system of symbols "stamping form onto" (ibid., 250) man's own experience, and the dependency model, which ignored the bond between sociopolitical thought--ideology--and cultural tradition, the Geertzian model of cultural interpretation of social change provides a clue to the conceptualization of the dialectic between persisting patterns of meaning and the concrete course of social life.

THE SOURCES, THE TIME FRAME, THE METHOD

In Russia between the 1890s and the 1930s, literature served as a replacement for those political, social, legal, and economic phenomena that could not develop fully in Russian society. Literary works and literary debates were seen by Russian writers as substitutes--if not complete, then at least symbolic--for those social activities whose normal manifestations were blocked by political, and perhaps also by psychological, difficulties. Artistic expression, stimulated by the troublesome feeling that Russia stood on the crossroads, exposed the moral and intellectual dilemmas of modernization in Russia.

I have chosen a wide spectrum of sources, ranging from the peasant wisdom of proverbs and folktales to the literary narratives, diaries, speeches, and sociopolitical and philosophical articles of the widely read and acclaimed Russian writers, thinkers, and revolutionaries, whose insights offer an avenue to a better understanding of the contemporary meaning of work. I investigate the Russian intelligentsia's perceptions of work in the literary narratives of Ivan Bunin, Anton Chekhov, Leonid Andreev, Maxim Gorky, Fedor Gladkov, Valentin Kataev, Anton Makarenko, Iurii Olesha, and Boris Pil'niak. The Christian intelligentsia's perceptions are represented in the diaries of Lev Tolstoy and the articles of the Christian philosophers Sergei Bulgakov and Nikolai Berdyayev. The Bolshevik vision of work is reflected in the speeches of the political leaders--Vladimir Lenin, Nikolai Bukharin, and Joseph Stalin.

In the controversy surrounding the Russian perception of work and social change, there can be discerned three distinct voices. The first is the Tolstoyan maxim of nonresistance to oppression, which I tentatively call the voice of surrender, the voice of the past. The second voice can be heard in the revolutionary maxim of struggle against the existing political and socioeconomic reality; it is the call for hope, which I call the voice of the future. Lurking behind those two maxims, the third voice, the voice of irony, is distinctly heard. It is the voice of doom, unable to see promise in past, present, or future.

That makes me pause for a while to expound on the rationale behind the chosen time frame. The year 1890 has been recognized by most experts as the beginning of Russian modernization.[10] In making the early

1930s cut-off point, I was guided by the desire not to venture into the period in Soviet history commonly known as the Great Purges. I believe the specificity of Stalin's dictatorship and the crucial changes in Soviet political and socioeconomic life that it brought about require independent research. The prerevolutionary (1890-1917) and postrevolutionary (1917-1932) periods warrant separate accounts.

Going back to the method, this much has to be stated in advance: in works of art, I look for the perceptions invoked by the images in the textual context. For what is gleaned is a comprehensive view of human activity as a mental extension of present possibilities. It was R. W. B Lewis who observed the ambiguous nature of narrative art which "inevitably and by nature invests its inherited intellectual content with a quickening duplicity. For the *experience* of the aims and values of an epoch is apt to be more complex and even more painful than the simple statements of them" (Lewis 1955, 3). That is not to ignore "the simple statements"--the proverbs--whose antagonistic or piously righteous tone suggest the peasant's ambiguity towards work. The crisp clarity of Tolstoy's, Berdyayev's, and Bulgakov's moral-philosophical maxims and Lenin's, Bukharin's, and Stalin's political credo, for all their unequivocal bias, offer a unique perspective on the cultural particularism of philosophical and political thinking.

The artistic narrative requires the method of textual analysis. In this exercise of teasing out the feelings and meanings the Russian attaches to his work, I use the method of textual analysis suggested by the anthropologist Clifford Geertz. To analyze, according to Geertz, is to "sort out the structures of signification" (Geertz 1973, 9) and "cast them in terms of the interpretation to which persons of a particular denomination [here the Russian] subject their experience" (ibid., 1973,15).

Given the overwhelming importance of religion in Russian pre-revolutionary life, in examining "the structures of signification" I have looked toward the Christian orthodoxy to provide the clues to its most cherished image--the passion of Christ. For at the turn of the century, both the Russian religious believer and atheist were nurtured by Christian biblical images. The puzzling combination of "the fury of unbelief" and "martyrdom" has been traced by an eminent Russian, Sergei Askol'dov, to the similarity between Christianity and socialism, since both are directed "toward the realization of someone else's political and social rights, not one's own" (Askol'dov 1986, 4). "Russia," Askol'dov writes, "already counts no small number of true religious martyrs for Christ and for the Church, who accepted a martyr's death from the fury of unbelief" (ibid., 31). Although the image of the sufferer was more explicit at the close of the nineteenth and in the first decade of the twentieth century than in the early twenties and thirties, it remained submerged, making itself felt in what Geertz called "a recommended attitude life, a recurrent mood, and a persistent set of motivations" (Geertz 1973, 124). Those moods and motivations leave their indelible imprint on secular life and account for the remarkable resilience and vitality of the image of the sufferer and the hero in Russia today.

The transmigration of the image of the Christian martyr into a communist martyr, from the Christian orthodox church to the Communist party pantheon, reveals something critically important about the Russian and the way he perceives himself in life. The celebration of readiness for suffering and sacrifice suggests a kind of ascetic labor, untouched and undefiled by mundane work, emancipated from history, and bereft of any familial and social attachments. The strong messianic message of universal salvation through suffering and sacrifice became closely identified with a heroic deed. It is not surprising for a culture as fervently attached to religion and its folklore as Russian culture to ultimately collapse the image of the religious sufferer into the image of the secular hero.

Such were the impulses which created the image of the sufferer and the hero. The perceptions it inspired and the ways those perceptions were negotiated by the changing social reality, as they were transposed, challenged and reaffirmed over the years, form the subject of this book.

In Part One, I explore the prerevolutionary perceptions of work: the contradictory mood of the imminent apocalypse and hope evoked by Russia's industrialization drive, which was accompanied by profound changes in urban and village social life; the institutionalization of police rule; and the sense among the public of the illegitimacy of the existing socioeconomic and political system. Following the rhythm of the interplay between the coercive official policies and growing public discontent, I examine and compare the perceptions of work among different representatives of the Russian cultural milieu. The central strain of work--the desire to exercise free will--acts as centrifugal force in the despotic and coercive social structure. The paradigm of man and authority, which in the context of Russian political reality was often seen as a question of life and death, has received different interpretation among different social groups.

I examine and compare the peasant's and the intellectual's conceptions of work in the interplay between man and authority. I review the peasant's and the intellectual's perceptions of ways of dealing with what they view as an oppressive and coercive environment. Mikhail Vrubel's painting *Demon Downcast*, interpreted in Chapter 2, which was widely popular when it was painted, represents the revolutionary intellectual's perception of work as defiance and challenge of the reigning authority. This rebellious mood is echoed in *To the Stars* by Andreev, and *Mother* by Gorky, the literary narratives discussed in Chapter 5, which were also highly acclaimed among Russian revolutionaries.

The roots of the peasant's perception of work are traced to his intimate experience of agricultural labor and his sense of identification with Christ's crucifixion. For the Russian word for peasant *(krestianin)* is etymologically linked to the word for cross *(krest),* and the peasant's primary activity, summer field work *(strada),* which also means "suffering," alludes to Christ's suffering on the cross. The interplay between the coercive environment and the peasant is explored in peasant lore--proverbs and folktales. The narratives reflect the perception of work which collapses the images of suffering into the art of escaping suffering through trickery and manipulation.

At the end of Part One, the peasant's folkloric and Vrubel's artistic representation of work are juxtaposed to reveal two vastly different perceptions. Unlike the peasant, the Russian intellectual--removed from the immediacy of the pain of physical labor and from the constraints imposed by the peasant communal life--extols direct confrontation and heroic defiance of death.

In Part One, I also examine the perceptions of prominent Russian thinkers on work and its relationship with Christian doctrine. The study of Tolstoy's diaries between 1890 and 1910 and the articles by Bulgakov and Berdyayev reveals a kinship of perceptions: the view of work as the means of personal and universal salvation. Tolstoy's celebration of altruistic work and his call for renunciation of the mundane life resonates in Bulgakov's deliberations on the virtues of ascetic labor and in Berdyayev's fierce insistence that the primary goal of work should be self-perfection. Thus the conception of freedom of will within the context of Tolstoy's, Bulgakov's, and Berdyayev's writings shifts the burden of work away from the interplay between man and authority to emphasize the individual's power to exercise his inner freedom of will in self-perfection and in accepting moral responsibility.

Chekhov's and Bunin's perceptions of work bellow with the sounds of fury at Tolstoy's celebration of suffering and renunciation of the mundane life. For all his acrimony, Chekhov shares with Tolstoy a strong aversion to pursuit of personal ambition and material gain that is other than socially useful, and so does Bunin. This censorship of material gain and pursuit of personal ambition suggests Russian Christian orthodoxy as a common source of cultural values. Seen from this perspective, work in the inimical social structure of Bunin's village and Chekhov's provincial town is seen as an exercise in futile ambition and eventual loss of hope. Unlike the peasant who sees his work as manipulating death and the revolutionary who defies it, Chekhov and Bunin announce surrender and welcome it as a reprieve from the curse of living.

The Russian's search for escape from the curse of being is examined on the routes expounded by Russian revolutionaries. The study of Andreev's *To the Stars* and Gorky's *Mother* suggests a shift in the Russian perception of work, and underlying it the image of the passion of Christ, from the celebration of suffering Christ to Christ the activist; from work as burden to work as heroic deed of self-sacrifice; from loss of hope to the glimmering glory of the kingdom on earth; from the man who is spiritless, anemic, and phlegmatic to the altruistic enthusiast.

In Part Two,. I elucidate "the moods and motivations" created by the Bolshevik revolution between 1917 and 1932. I explore the Bolsheviks' visions of work in what they perceived as the dawn of communism. Lenin's ideas of work are revealed in his speeches, while his letters betray his diminishing sense of hope in changing the Russian's attitude to work. The Bolsheviks' desire to animate their vision of communist work through reinvigorated class conscience are revealed in Bukharin's speeches. Stalin's skillful exploitation of the Russian penchant to revere symbols is examined in the nascent movement to infuse the conception of work with the new symbolism that merged the Russian and the Western conceptions of work. I investigate how the Bolshevik vision of work is interpreted by widely acclaimed contemporary writers. I examine the restored sense of hope in the process of appropriation and affirmation of the charismatic heroic figure which is epitomized by the socialist worker.

I deal with the mood of disappointment and hopelessness in Iurii Olesha's *Zavist'* (Envy) and Boris Pil'niak's *Mahogany*. I explore the final co-optation of the ironic to reveal the collapse of the two maxims into one in the recurrent sense of disenchantment with either past, present, or future.

In the end, I draw some conclusions about the Russian perceptions of work. Unless we find the means to shake the image of the sufferer and the hero from its choleric swings from the extreme of surrender into the extreme of sacrifice and provide it with the sense of value in the perhaps inglorious, but nonetheless vitally important steady and protracted mundane work, there is a mortal danger for the country's fledgling democracy. In this respect, the review of the image helps to chart the way in reeducating the Russian public, particularly, the young. However perilously misleading the image of suffering has been, it has, nonetheless, stimulated a positive and original sense of heroic sacrifice, as well as active identification with a sense of change. Without this illusion, the Russians would have been left not with a sense of pathos and drama, but with a sterile awareness of doldrums and depravity. To eradicate the illusion is to surrender to the sense of despair and cynicism flaunted by contemporary Russian social and literary life.

Part One

The Modality of Suffering and Heroism

1

The Case against the Present

What is it? A new cloud with the gilded edges? Is it a far and a deceptive illusion that at a close look turns into a cold darkness, or is it a
thunderstorm cloud? It doesn't matter! It is life! From the cloud comes
rain, which waters the earth, and the thunderstorm, which clears the
air.

--Vladimir Korolenko, *S Dvukh Storon*

Three decades after the abolition of serfdom in 1861, the air of an
impending storm became apparent in Russian life and letters. Many a
Russian shared a profound sense of change about the situation in the
country, the change that bore in it the seeds of the total destruction of the
existing political and socioeconomic order. The feeling of the imminent
apocalypse and the ray of hope it cast were enunciated in two seemingly
polar visions of universal salvation: one looked to the future, the other
embodied a nostalgia for the past, a desire to return to the utopian
peasant commune. The vision of universal salvation was eloquently
symbolized by the metaphor of the rejuvenating thunderstorm and biblical
flood. The visions of suffering and of heroic deeds received their
metaphoric representations in the Christian symbolism of the passion of
Christ. Whether it was one vision or the other, all converged on a
common ground: the existing structure had to be demolished and erased.
An acute observer could not escape the visible signs of inevitable doom.

The drive to industrialize Russia, chartered and monitored at the tsarist
bureaucratic top, deracinated millions of peasants. The dilapidated
shantytowns around the newly-built factories arising in the suburbs,
covered by dirt and soot from the belching factory chimneys, became the

centers of feverish revolutionary unrest. The rancid factory barracks were teaming with peasants turned into migrant workers, whose shared experience and shared lodgings inadvertently created a potent explosive brew of growing self-awareness and anger.[1]

Another pivotal factor in the growing revolutionary activities was the proliferation of public universities, which produced an educated group whose numbers far exceeded the needs of the fledgling capitalist enterprises.[2] The university-educated professionals, unable to find employment or any other outlet for their mind and talent, felt betrayed by the system, which refused them an access to active participation in the existing power structure.

The fervent tempo of industrialization and the unprecedented growth of railroads and heavy industry was marked by gross disregard for agriculture. Heavy taxation plunged the countryside into deep paroxysms of hunger and violent outbursts of peasant ire. The poetic lament of an anonymous peasant-poet spoke of life as bondage and bemoaned the betrayed trust in religious and secular authority.

We work, we labor in the sweat of our brow
But we still can't afford even an egg for the Holy Day.
We share our chaff with the horses.
Lest our women are idle
They tax each household
With half a pound of flax.
The Christian belief is no longer there.
The judges have become unjust,
The priests are drunkards.
They have laid a heavy tribute on the people.[3]

For all Russian industrialization, the peasant turned migrant worker remained anchored in the village commune and the village way of life. Until Petr Stolypin's reforms of 1905, the peasant was legally tied to the commune and obliged to pay its taxes and fees and was unable to leave the village without permission from the commune and the head of his family. "After the emancipation," an astute student of the Russian peasantry, Moshe Lewin, observes, "they [the peasants] were enmeshed in a triple harness: the *obshchestvo* (the commune), state officialdom, and the fetters associated with the patriarchal family system" (Lewin 1985, 74).

The industrialization process carried out by decree and burdened by taxes and controls was mired by the "institutionalization of police rule" (Crankshaw 1976, 272) and the growing sense among the public of the illegitimacy of the existing political and socioeconomic system. The mood of the people, which ranged from profound despair to the giddy heights of hope, seemingly carried the country to an apocalyptic crash envisioned by the optimists as a poetic, revitalizing thunderstorm. A prominent social-democrat, ethnographer, and historian of the Russian sectarian movement, Vladimir Bonch-Bruevich, listened with pleasure to the Russian sectarian's talk about the approaching salvation. In 1902 in the emigre journal *Zhizn'*, he cited with open glee a sectarian predicting that "the rumblings of the approaching thunderstorm would turn into a storm of an immense destructive power." It would usher, the sectarian insisted, "the light of the new day, when every living being, young and strong, will breathe freely, will celebrate the exciting life, and in a powerful thrust will create a wonderful, free, and happy life" (Bonch-Bruevich 1902, 6:251).

The metaphor of the thunderstorm among those who hoped for revolution revealed the convergence of two sets of perceptions that contributed to the revolutionary mood and experience--those of Christians and those of ethnic Russians. The Christian symbolism was rooted in the psychological identification of revolution with the biblical flood, and the ethnic one manifested the Russian's sense of unity with nature and drew its analogies from natural phenomena.

It was the continuing process of negotiation between Christian and ethnic Russian symbolism and the intensifying political struggle which gave rhythm and shape to the Russian response to industrialization and revolution. Both the religious and ethnic representations of storm were intimately bound with Russian celebration of violent change as a means of universal salvation. The storm and its biblical inference had a ritualistic quality, and much of the rhythm of Bonch-Bruevich's piece was sustained in the tone of prophetic oratory. Behind the image of the flood, we see the deeply ingrained human desire for rebirth, highlighted by Bonch-Bruevich's metaphors: "the new day, young, strong, powerful."

To conclude, in his censorship of the present, the Russian articulated his perception of work within the context of Russian industrialization, which was marked by persisting despotic police rule, a heavy tax burden upon the peasantry, and limited access for the intelligentsia to participate in the existing power structure. The Russian perceptions of work, enunciated in the visions of salvation from the odium of the present, represented the interplay between the Christian image of the passion of Christ, the ethnic sense of unity with nature, and contemporary socioeconomic and political reality. The Russian case against the present received particular poignancy in the ethnic perception of work as man's response to the conflict between him and coercive authority. The Russian's interpretation of the double message of the conflict--defeat and victory--yields illuminating insights into the peasant's and the intellectual's conceptions of response to coercion, negotiated by the Christian image of the passion of Christ.

2

The Poetics of Defeat and Victory: Ivan the Fool and the Demon Downcast

The Russian preoccupation with the passion of Christ and its image, which is deeply etched in the folk memory, has been the source and the end result of the Russian historical experience, or what Anthony Giddens has succinctly called "the circular activity" (Giddens 1987, 163). In this chapter, I explore the interplay of the image and the social reality in the semantic paradigm of the Russian concept of *suffering*: the conflation of the spiritual and the mundane, of the ecclesiastical image and summer agricultural work. Insofar as the peasant recognized suffering as an intrinsic part of his social being and work as a continuous test of his endurance and wit, the intellectual tended to view suffering in more abstract terms of confrontation between man and authority. The peasant folklore and Mikhail Vrubel's *Demon Downcast* enunciate, first, the folk and, second, the artistic perceptions of purposeful activity in the con-temporary historic context.

Unlike the intellectual, whose sense of crucifixion was divorced from the immediacy of physical pain, the peasant had a perception that was strongly colored by the intimate experience of physical pain associated with agricultural work. This connection between religious suffering and value attached to work by the Russian peasant is evident in the semantic meaning of the Russian word for peasant (*krestianin*). The root of the noun *krest* (the cross) invokes Christ carrying the cross on his way to Golgotha and a sense of partaking alongside Jesus Christ in the same torment of suffering. The peasant experience amplified this sense of identification with the suffering Christ to include the most vital period of agricultural cycle--the summer field work. Crop gathering, which was associated with backbreaking work and with death (the death of the plant), bore the seeds of the promise of future life--the simulacrum of Christ's suffering, his painful death on the cross, and the promise of resurrection. The identification of the peasant with Christ's suffering is clear in Russian folktales and popular aphorisms.

The Russians, being predominantly agricultural people, gave *strada* (summer fieldwork) an ambiguous meaning which combined a sense of reverence with loafing. V. I. Dal's dictionary of the Russian language (1909) identified the Russian word for *strada* as "hard, backbreaking work," "various kinds of *suffering*," and "the process of *dying*." What we witness here is the conscious convergence between the peasant's image of physical suffering as the result of hard work and the spiritual image of physical and mental suffering before the crucifixion. Thus, the cyclical relation between the actual peasant experience and the ecclesiastical image nurtured and sustained the Russian peasant's love-hate vision of his work as life-giving and life-taking.

This familiar discord lent its tone and rhythm of self-effacing contradictory values to a number of Russian popular aphorisms, such as "work is bitter, but bread is sweet" *("gor'ka rabota da khleb sladok")* (Dal' 1984, 2:19) or "work is dirty, but money is not" *("rabota cherna, da denezhka bela")* (ibid.). The omnipresent conjunctive "but" signals the rupture in the rhythm, the juxtaposition of two mutually effacing notions, embedded in the use of antonyms, such as "bitter" vs. "sweet" or "black" vs. "white."

But it would be a gross simplification to reduce the perception of physical work to a mere "love-hate" relationship, for as I have already mentioned, there is a message of hope embedded both in the mundane and the spiritual experiences--the hope of resurrection. From this vantage point, the juxtaposition of opposites could imply the promise of dialectic movement: that defeat carried the seeds of victory, as suffering in the agricultural cycle is pregnant with rebirth (the harvested seeds will bear future fruits).

The collapse of opposites, manifested in the collusion of the mundane and the spiritual, the negative and the positive, defeat and victory, reveals the peasant's conscious attempt to find a leverage in dealing with the otherwise destructive experience, for example the exorbitant tax burden imposed on the peasant and the existing legal system, which violated the peasant's conception of the right of labor and the right to labor. The right of labor postulated that land belonged to those who tilled it, and, therefore, the present landowners had no legal rights to the land. The right to labor meant the peasant's primordial right to exist and to subsist and, hence, the right to a land allotment, which justified, in case of land shortage, expropriation from the landowner.

It is within the context of peasant hostility to outside authority, which violated his sense of law, animosity, repressed hatred, and an intense belief in heavenly justice, enunciated in Christ's martyrdom, that we should interpret the hero's actions in Russian folktales.

In *Kuplennaya Devushka* (*The Purchased Maiden*), recorded in 1912 (Smirnov 1917, 25-38), the hero, Ivan, the son of a distinguished merchant, loses his father, and has to provide for his mother and himself. The merchants of the town take pity on the family and offer him a good deal, which would keep Ivan's family comfortable. Once, when he has very little money left, Ivan buys with it a maiden. The maiden turns out to be a gift from heaven, as she can do wonderful embroidery. The tsar gets so enamored with her work that he opens his coffers to Ivan and declares him his sworn brother. No longer compassionate, the envious merchants incite the tsar to send Ivan on an impossible mission: to obtain *gusli* (a three-stringed musical instrument) that they can play on their own. The punishment for failure promises to be a swift and merciless "off with your head!" Helped out by his wife, Ivan finds the place where *gusli* are made. It turns out that the strings are made from human sinews, which are pulled from a person who is crucified (*raspiat*) for that purpose. Ivan is ordered to supervise the procedure lest it go wrong and the person is wasted if Ivan falls asleep. Ivan does fall asleep, but, ironically, waste is inevitable--the warehouse is full of *gusli*.

Leached out of the sublime suffering of crucifixion, the torture is presented as comic waste: "Had you told me earlier [that you needed *the gusli*], I would not have had to waste this man" (ibid., 32). In the end, Ivan avenges himself on the tsar and the merchants. He returns to the kingdom flanked by a powerful army and beheads everyone who happens to be in his way, including the tsar and the merchants. "They chopped off the heads, and they crucified whoever they suspected bore a grudge against them" (ibid., 38).

The mocking laughter accompanying the scene of violence, in the conspicuous presence of the act of crucifixion, unsettles the ethos of crucifixion with its deeply ingrained sense of the noble purpose and pathos of suffering and salvation. The image of hope, then, is effaced in ridicule. The act of crucifixion, as the tale reveals, is devoid of reason.

There are other folktales which reveal the range of perceptions generated in the process of negotiation between the modernizing society and its largest socioeconomic group. The peasant's sense of helplessness and anguish in the face of the erosion of his means of livelihood was manifested in the folkloric image of free will released from the bondage of earthly life. It is the deep sense of irony bursting in burlesque belly laughter that keeps the balance between the fantasy world of the tale and grim reality. The passage from the tale *Soldat i Smert'* (Soldier and Death), recorded in 1914 (ibid., 577-82), will serve as an example.

The story is about a soldier who, upon completing his lengthy term of service, returns to his native village to find out that none of his family are alive. There is nowhere for him to go. God takes pity on him because "the soldier is a good person" (ibid., 577) and assigns him to guard the entrance to paradise. The soldier is disappointed and feels betrayed when he discovers that paradise is worse than his earthly life. While on guard, the soldier is taunted by bitter frost. Let inside the paradise to warm himself up, he is warned lest he smoke or drink a glass of wine and defile the sacred place. Disgusted, the soldier returns to his post and takes matters into his own hands. When Death arrives to consult with God on impending victims, the soldier dispatches her on different humiliating assignments. His tricks exposed, the soldier is banished from paradise. The experience teaches the soldier a very important lesson: if he can manipulate God and Death with ease, then manipulating people, who have more than a fair share of gullibility, will present no problem. The soldier does indeed prosper, but he is no longer the master of his fate. His wealth--his land and crops--now control his life. His wealth turns him into a hapless pawn in the comic rivalry between two saints. Ultimately the soldier extricates himself from a tricky situation when he artfully ingratiates himself with one of the saints.

The deflated image of paradise is devoid of the basic "joys" the Russian peasant entertains. "The smoke and the hearty drink" mock the popular image of the heavenly kingdom and, with it, obliterate and ridicule the sense of hope. With the hope of future bliss gone, what is perceived as the only viable option left, the only means of survival, is manipulation, trickery, and conniving. That is the essence of the soldier's victory over Death and the saint.

At the same time, however, the tale reveals another mood--the mood of harmony with nature. What we have witnessed in the tale is an intimate acquaintance with an anthropomorphic God, one who is no stranger to compassion (when he assigns the soldier to guard paradise) as well as wrath (when he banishes the soldier from paradise).

The soldier's shuttling between heaven and earth betrays the same collapse of two realities as does the notion of "suffering" and reaffirms the desacralization of the heavenly kingdom. The soldier's final victory, mediated by the benevolent St. Nicholas, devalues and deglamorizes the soldier's work, which is explicitly represented in his abundant crops, and shifts the emphasis from his power to his manipulation and deceit. The arbitrariness and volatility of human life is explicitly conveyed in the celebration of the soldier's defeats and victories.

The hero's survival and manipulation and deceit are also evident in another folktale *Neznaiko* (The One That Doesn't Know), recorded in 1912 (ibid., 58-68). Tsarevich Ivan is introduced as the paragon of the heroic personality. The metaphors for "mighty"-- *bogatyrskii* and *buinyi* (unruly, tempestuous)--allude to a belief in the consummate unity between heroism and free will. The carnivalesque description of Ivan's forays into the city, where he wreaks death and havoc among the inhabitants, is analogous to the pattern of behavior of the Ivan in *The Purchased Maiden*. Inasmuch as senseless violence is represented as farce, which Vladimir Propp, an eminent student of Russian folklore called "poetic fiction" (Propp 1984, 19), it is the obvious lack of motive and provocation in both tales that paradoxically strengthens the comic representation of acts of mutilation. Now we will go back to the tale and see it through to its end. Ivan arrives in a different kingdom and feigns stupidity (this assumed foolishness is his tool for manipulating the unknown environment). Assigned to the kitchen, Ivan at first suffers in silence the cook's bossing him around. Unseen by anyone, he sheds off his veneer of a dunce and is transformed into his old self--a mighty hero--and goes on a rampage. "If he snatches anyone by the hand, off goes that hand; if he snatches the head, off it comes!" (Smirnov 1917, 59-60) Bored to death, he mounts his mighty horse and destroys the tsar's garden. Having "let off steam" he goes back to acting as a fool: he rides his horse backward and then skins it alive. Called upon to defend the kingdom, Ivan, his old self, scores three victories, wins the crown, and becomes the tsar.

The persistence of the pattern of comic violence in both "Ivan" folktales is leveled against faceless victims, whose very lack of individuality serves as a metaphor for a larger social unit. It is this social unit that has to be violated before victory can be declared. The laughter, or to be more precise the paradox of laughter, deemphasizes the human element in the victims, makes the grotesqueness of the butchery vaudeville-like, and, finally, effaces any sensitivity and feeling of moral outrage. There is a direct correlation between violence in the folktales and the violence which was gripping the country: hunger rebellions, the bloody events of the 1905 revolution, and the ignominious defeat in the Russo-Japanese War of 1904-5.

The question of cultural mediation requires another close look at the narratives. The Ivan of the first folktale did not have to conceal his identity because he was not the *tsarevich*, the prince. But the Ivan in the second tale was the *tsarevich*, and a disguise *was needed* when he arrived into an alien environment. He assumed the role of a dunce to protect his true identity as a noble. The narrative suggests that heroic deeds can be committed only by a noble, and the role of a dunce is allotted to the servant who is the peasant. However, it is not the dunce, but the noble, who wreaks death to affirm his power and his control over the kingdom. Ironically, the dunce's cruelty is a travesty of the *tsarevich's cruelty*: the tsarevich kills the people, the dunce "skins the horse alive."

From this perspective, Ivan's quest is an obvious act of challenge to and humiliation of the power of the reigning authority, whereby everything more or less associated with the existing authority is scourged, mutilated, and extinguished. Within this context, the peasant's laughter is subversive. The grotesque comic violence against the deindividualized crowd, the mutilated, and hacked-to-death faceless multitude, dehumanizes the victims and accepts and recognizes violence as an integral part of human activity in the authoritative structure.

The capping irony of all Russian folktales is the narrator's obvious inability to satiate his hunger and thirst amidst the abundance of the victorious feast. His complaint, "I was there, drank honey and beer; it rolled down my mustache, but it did not get into my mouth," mocks and effaces any sense of hope, whatever change might occur, deprives the folk perception of the peasant's work of a sense of promise for happiness. With the sense of hope gone and suffering part of his identity, the peasant, in his feverish search to alleviate the pain of being, celebrates Ivan the Fool and his trove of tricks to manipulate the hostile environment.

Insofar as the peasant identified with the physical suffering of Christ, the intellectual, removed from the pain of physical suffering, looked toward the psychological and moral message in the passion of Christ. It was Mikhail Vrubel' who, in *Demon Downcast* (1902), gave artistic expression to his own perception of suffering.

For Vrubel', whose *Demon Downcast* was painted as the apotheosis of defiance against the authority of God, the Demon did not carry the stigma of evil usually associated with Lucifer. In *Demon Downcast*, the crucial distinctions between the two realities--the rebellion and the fall--collided to celebrate the duality of human experience. Vrubel's own acknowledgement that the Demon was "the spirit that is not so much evil as suffering and grieving" (Kaplanova 1975, 55) laid the emphasis on the intrinsically Russian value of suffering, in contrast to the Western preoccupation with good and evil (Lucifer).

The painting shows a smashed body sprawled listlessly on razor-sharp rocks amidst the hostile fury of the elements. The intensity of colors in Vrubel's palette, violet-blue against the golden hue of broken wings, is accentuated by the intensity of brush strokes molding the lines of the body and of the landscape. The body, emaciated and broken with a sharply protruding rib cage and bone-thin arms convulsively twisted upward in the agony of utter desperation, is set against the gushing vehemence of the waves and the dark, broken lines of mute rocks. The visual conceptualization of the lethal crash and the air of despondency and hopelessness hovering in the background evokes the artists's profound sense of sympathy for the victim.

What is poignant and powerful about Vrubel's representation of the *Demon Downcast* is that it can be interpreted as signifying both the tragedy of dissent and the harsh celebration of defiance. Vrubel' conjured up a punishment so severe that the image of suffering obliterated what would otherwise be celebrated as the victory of good over evil. We have here Vrubel's emphatic affirmation that Demon's defiance of divine authority represented the convergence of the sublime and the base, good and evil--the essence of being human. It may be that Vrubel' in his own rite of salvation was consciously seeking to bring out in this painting his own inner perception of man's relation with authority and to celebrate defiance unmitigated by the severe pain of the punishment. The rite of salvation, the passion of Christ, reconciles two opposites: Christ's surrender (his willing acquiescence to his terrible lot) and the celebration of Christ's spiritual victory. This convergence is not only obvious in Vrubel's painting, but it is manifest in literature that rhapsodizes religious suffering and self-sacrifice and in literature that condemns and extols revolution.

To conclude, if we juxtapose two perceptions of the fall from grace and suffering--the artist's and the peasant's--we observe a difference in the interpretation of defeat between the artist-intellectual Vrubel' and the folk mind. Where Vrubel's Demon when downcast is deprived of a sense of victory, the soldier of the folktale, cast out from the paradise, is given the chance to *manipulate* his victory. But the Demon's fall, by virtue of association with the passion of Christ, wears a badge of honor and celebrates the individual and his defiance against commonly accepted authority. The peasant, however, having acknowledged his own insignificance and inability to measure up to authority, consciously effaces the heroic. Thus he leaves himself two choices: ever "to be slaughtered," that is to metaphorically surrender to arbitrary rule, or to manipulate his way out. The negotiation between the sublime (the passion of Christ) and the mundane (agricultural work), the recurrent act of interplay of collusion and differentiation, accounts for a deep sense of irony evoked in the deadly game of survival. It is within the context of survival in a hostile environment of arbitrary and volatile rule that we can understand and relate to the peasant's perception of work as trickery and deceit, which sets him apart from the intellectual, who seeks the perfect and the absolute in salvation.

3

The Function of Religion:
Tolstoy, Bulgakov, Berdyayev

Therefore I tell you, do not be anxious about your life, what you shall eat and what you shall drink, not about your body, what you shall put on.

Matthew 6:25

Apart from the realm of the physical work of the peasant and the turbulent artistic search for individual expression, the Russian meaning of work at the turn of the century got its expression in the religious-philosophical maxims of Lev Tolstoy, Sergei Bulgakov, and Nikolai Berdyayev--the renowned Russian thinkers of that time. Lev Tolstoy, who according to A. N. Wilson was "one of the most notable of nineteenth century Russian dissidents, one whom both the Government and, subsequently, Lenin recognized as more than half-doing the revolutionary's work for them" (Wilson 1988, 40-41), looked to the passion of Christ as a guide to moral and meaningful work. Tolstoy's plea for altruistic work of self-sacrifice and for a return to the religious fold echoed what in the words of a perceptive chronicler of the Russian cultural scene, V. Zenkovsky, was a "revolutionary or reforming movement" under the aegis of a new "religious consciousness."[1] Tolstoy sought "to rationalize from the life and teaching of Jesus, the man, a satisfying prescription for human behavior and the establishment of the kingdom of heaven on earth" (Christian 1969, 213). Likewise, the Russian Christian intelligentsia, with Bulgakov and Berdyayev in its forefront, envisioned a return to religion, to the ethical values of the passion of Christ, as the only viable alternative to the corrosive powers of European modernization and "bourgeois civilization," which substituted the man of the spirit with "the automated man."[2] The Christian intelligentsia loathed capitalist civilization, which "has developed powerful technical forces, meant to prepare the kingdom of man over nature--but whose technical forces control the man himself, enslave him, murder his soul."[3]

The Russian intelligentsia's proclivity to seek moral guidance in religion, in the life advocated by Jesus, "the progress from artist to sage or holy man," has been, in Wilson's words, "fairly common among Russian writers. Gogol did it. In his own fashion, Dostoyevsky did it. We have the contemporary example of Solzhenitsyn" (Wilson 1988, 301).

The Russian revolutions of 1905 and 1917 set off a powerful explosion of soul-searching and self-flagellation. Not only did the members of the Christian intelligentsia feel their expectations for liberal reforms and redemption betrayed, but they also became acutely aware and fearful of the uncontrollable destructive powers those revolutions had unleashed. These Russian Christian intellectuals attacked the moral assumptions and what they regarded as the dogmatic presumptuousness of the Russian revolutionary intelligentsia. Their commentaries may serve as a prologue to inspecting the Bolshevik version of the passion and its interpretations by Russian Soviet writers. Because the program of the Russian Christian intellectuals was Russian Orthodox in temper, they felt that the revolutionary heroic deed and revolutionary self-sacrifice, even if deeply religious in their roots, nonetheless represented a flagrant perversion of Christian faith. Viewing the world from their own Orthodox Christian perspective, Russian Christian intellectuals preached a return to God and salvation through suffering. The Christian intellectuals' stern repudiation of the Russian revolutionaries revealed the perennial Russian Orthodox impulse toward inner perfection and otherworldliness. The Christian intellectuals were determined to perform the classical function of Russian Orthodoxy--to show the Russians the way to the heavenly kingdom--and to speak the truth as they perceived it.

The first salvo of the attack was *Vekhi* (*The Signposts*) (1909), a collection of articles on the Russian revolutionary intellectuals' system of beliefs and their cultural origins. Jolted by the savagery of the 1905 revolution, the authors of *Vekhi* blamed the failure of the revolution, and its violence, on the Russian intelligentsia's inherent inability to deal with social reality, on its misunderstanding and mishandling of the Russian penchant for anarchy. If in their attempts to ward off future disaster the authors of *Vekhi* sounded like Biblical prophets, their criticism and suggested remedy, ironically, exhibited their kinship with the revolutionary intelligentsia in their common disregard for social reality and basic human needs.

In *Iz Glubiny* (*Out of the Depths*) (1918), some of the Russian Christian intellectuals reflected on the lessons of the Bolshevik revolution. The somber apocalyptic title from the opening of Psalm 130, "Out of the depths have I cried unto thee, O Lord," set the tone of the articles. The prophets of Russian doom surveyed the debris of their tumbled familiar world, explored once more the source of Russia's evil-- the revolutionary intelligentsia's moral and political values--and pointed out the road to Russia's redemption. Redemption, the authors of *Vekhi* and *Iz Glubiny* believed, could be achieved only through a return to Russian spiritual roots, to Russian Orthodoxy.

For the purpose of the present study, I have chosen those authors who discuss the role and the place of religious symbolism in the Russian intelligentsia's paradigm of perceptions. The major voices in the assaults on the Russian revolutionary intelligentsia's perceptions of purposeful human activity belonged to Sergei Bulgakov and Nikolai Berdyayev. The latter denounced the revolutionary intelligentsia's appropriation of the passion of Christ image and the sense of righteousness that accompanied this act of appropriation.

In order to combat the pretensions of righteousness, the Christian intelligentsia found it necessary, first of all, to re-establish what they took to be the true nature of Russian Orthodoxy. The central issues of human work, in their minds, could be resolved only in religious terms; in terms, that is, of the relation between man's activity and God. Bulgakov saw self-perfection through the rigors of Christian asceticism as the only means of salvation. Berdyayev, on the other hand, propounded personal moral responsibility as the supreme resource of redemption.

In taking the pulse of the Russian Christian intelligentsia's perceptions of work at the turn of the century, its intrinsic link to Russian Orthodox religion, and its ethos of the passion of Christ, I find useful to begin with Lev Tolstoy (1828-1910), whose life, Wilson suggests, "could be read as an heroic attempt to live as Jesus Christ told his followers that they should live" (Wilson 1988, 300). Born into Russian nobility, Tolstoy was orphaned at a very early age. Perhaps it was his early encounter with death, combined with the horrors of the senseless butchery he witnessed during the Crimean War and the deaths of his two brothers and five of his thirteen children, which kept him on a constant quest for the transcendental. Wrecked by the pain of those losses, he sought feverishly for the meaning of life away from the mundane life, fraught with trampled hope and crushed ambition. By the late 1870s, after a long journey through military exploits, literary fame, and love, Tolstoy's spiritual crisis reached its zenith. From that time on, faith, as he understood it, became his only refuge from an otherwise meaningless life. In his *Confession* of 1882, he admitted that "only faith which is unreasonable makes life possible" (Christian 1969, 216). Tolstoy's rhapsodizing about faith was, in Christian's able observation, "groping . . . [for] a moral life, the sanction for which was to be at least in part the precepts and example of Christ" (ibid., 217).

Bent on transcending the pain of social and material reality, Tolstoy believed that work, driven by human ambition and self-interest, was not only tortuous, but harmful and sacrilegious. On September 12, 1889, he enunciated his credo of the virtue of altruistic work in his diary:

> The purpose of life's activity is to rejoice. Take precautions not to dis-rupt happiness. Avoid labor for yourself, tortuous labor. Activity for others is not labor. What a terrible delusion of our world to consider work, labor virtuous. Neither this nor that, it is rather a vice. Christ did not work (Tolstoy 1965, 19:392).

On his occasional visits to Moscow from his estate in Iasnaia Poliana, Tolstoy watched with a weary eye the swelling city, bursting with commotion and festering with human greed and ambition. Tolstoy loathed modern science and industrial technology, which he believed perpetuated a more sophisticated and cruel form of slavery. On April 10, 1890, he pondered in his diary over the evils of capitalist greed and gave voice to his wrenching doubts about the promise of modernization:

> As long as there is coercion, the force of capitalism and invention has been diverted. While a small part benefits from civilization, the great majority is deprived of its benefits. Whatever the increase in the good, those on the top use all of it for themselves . . . luxury has no limits . . . the increase in productivity, increasing control over nature, plays into the hands of the wealthy classes. The ruling class provides them with the leverage to retain all the benefits and control over the work-ing classes (ibid., 19:418).

In his enchantment with the Russian peasant and his nostalgia for the peasant's mythical communal way of life, Tolstoy refused to succumb to the Populists'[4] disillusionment with the idea of achieving social change through peasant education. While some Populists embraced the Marxist idea of violent political change and others navigated towards religious orthodoxy, Tolstoy, according to E. J. Simmons, "was well advanced on the path of his own revolution" (Simmons 1946, 10). His was the revolution of the spirit, a "moral revolution" (ibid., 15). When the converts to Marxist revolution reveled in the visions of the impending revitalizing thunderstorm and the new society created on its ruins, Tolstoy, intensely alert to the illusory nature of man-made institutions and social arrangements, warned lest men substitute one form of yoke, the monarchist order, with another, the capitalist. Looking in rapture at his friend Nikolai Ge's painting *What is Truth* (1890), which depicted the harried Christ who after the night of judgement and suffering faces the contemptuous, majestic Pontius Pilate, Tolstoy saw in it the "the moral significance of Christ's life and teaching" (Wilson 1988, 409). "Ge has found a moment in Christ's life," Tolstoy wrote, "which is important for all of us now and which is repeated everywhere throughout the world--in the struggle of the moral, rational consciousness of a man making himself manifest in the humdrum realities of life" (ibid.).

For Tolstoy, the image of the passion of Christ was the epitome of man's work. Christ's voluntary self-sacrifice was the bold act of asserting the role of individual moral choice in the fate of mankind. On July 16, 1905, Tolstoy gave voice to his conviction in his diary: "To be heard by the people one has to be ready to sacrifice oneself, to endure suffering, even better--death" (Tolstoy 1965, 20:152). Christ's willing surrender was, Tolstoy insisted, the hallmark of spiritual victory.

There was, and I suspect the effect was intended, a shock value in those lines. Tolstoy enunciated his maxim without resorting to any symbolic language, and the explicitness of his proposition brings to the fore two critical issues pertinent to this discussion. First is the question of the viability of his proposition, for the extreme position Tolstoy takes is at sharp variance with his immediate social environment and with the historical period. Tolstoy appropriated his maxim from the time of early Christianity, when it was at odds with the rest of society. Tolstoy's call for sacrifice challenged the existing social order and its stalwart, the Orthodox Church. The nature of Tolstoy's polemics against the official Church is beyond the scope of this research. Suffice it here to quote G. W. Spence, who claims that Tolstoy's criticism of the Orthodox Church was caused by his sense of "disgust by its [the Orthodox Church's] practices and doctrine" (Spence 1968, 13).

Like St. Matthew, Tolstoy took on the role of the prophet and Christ's disciple. The transposition of the experience of the persecuted first Christians into twentieth century Russia manifested Tolstoy's purpose, which was to challenge the existing social structure and reveal its oppressive and corrupt nature. This was a sentiment analogous to the peasant's lamentation cited in chapter six. The explosive power of the proposition, reminiscent of the ardent optimism of the first Christians, was intrinsically rooted in such ritualistic events as the passion of Christ. Tolstoy emphasized the value of spiritual work over any other kind of purposeful human activity.

For Tolstoy, the question of purposeful human activity was intrinsically linked to the notion of moral choice. He vehemently protested against attempts to extol the virtues of work, which would serve to perpetuate the yoke of social control in the inherently restrictive society. A staunch believer in moral choice and an opponent of social and religious institutions, Tolstoy was irked by Emile Zola, who in his *Speech to Youth* exhorted young people to embrace science and hard work. Alexander Dumas's response to the speech, however, expressed in a letter written to a French newspaper, struck a resonant chord in Tolstoy's soul. Unlike Zola, Dumas counseled young people to base their lives and activities on brotherly love. Tolstoy attacked Zola's celebration of science and its rationalization of the virtuousness of work in the essay *Ne Delanie* (Non-Acting) (1897).[5] Tolstoy argued that the contemporary infatuation with agnosticism and adulation of science represented a fallacious assumption that science could become, instead of religion, a new panacea for mankind.

Tolstoy used the speech by Zola and the letter by Dumas as a fulcrum to explicate his own ideal of the altruistic deed, which he strained to distance from the notion of labor. Tolstoy perceived the difference between labor and altruistic deed as psychological, rather than physical. Working for oneself meant labor, working for others was an altruistic deed, "activity for the other is not labor" (Tolstoy 1897, 14:22). Tolstoy remained faithful to the Russian past and the Orthodox belief expounded by St. Niphon, who had asserted in *Izmaragd*, a book for the laity in ancient Russia, that "nobody is saved by pleas, men are saved or condemned by deeds" (Fedotov 1946, 49). As for scientific truths, Tolstoy thundered, those held as true and sacred in the present were in danger of being rendered questionable by future generations, which would expose the fallacy of the ideology of work espoused by Zola. For Tolstoy, both science and the Puritan work ethic sought to surrender individual moral judgement to the dictates of external social authority. "The mysticism in religion and the stupefying effect of labor on science are equally deceptive. Both are superstitions, one from the past and the other one from the present" (Tolstoy 1897, 14:19).

Trying to conform with his moral choice of following the path of Christ and his belief in the saving value of the altruistic deed, Tolstoy, according to E. J. Simmons, dispensed with his aristocratic title of "Count," dressed in peasant-style clothes, and gave up his beloved hunting, liquor, meat, and smoking. The aristocrat with a retinue of servants cleaned his own room, cut wood, drew water, and even made his own boots, after taking lessons from a shoemaker (Simmons 1946, 126). He strove to go beyond pure rhetoric and mere vision. He put his ideas to work for the benefit of others. The experience of plowing the widow's field, cleaning his own room, and making his own boots strengthened his inner conviction that self-abnegating physical work offered itself as the best path toward the liberation of the spirit. True happiness, Tolstoy believed, lay in exercising one's moral choice, which was commonly hampered by mundane desires. "The exhaustion and pain in the muscles after hard physical work," asserted Tolstoy, gives a person "freedom from temptations, . . . real happiness" (Tolstoy 1897, 14:23).

In Tolstoy's moral-philosophical teaching, altruistic physical labor transcended the purely biological, life-sustaining function and acquired the function of a cleansing agent--*anestezicheskoe sredstvo* (anaesthesia)-- against vice and the corruption of contemporary society. It created favorable conditions for "the satisfaction of the individual's spiritual needs" (ibid.). Hence everything associated with the present and industrialization, including the Puritan celebration of industriousness, were perceived by Tolstoy as ploys to coerce people to work harder and to limit their free will.

Tolstoy mellowed when, upon returning from the hustle and bustle of Moscow to his permanent abode in Iasnaia Poliana, he looked around at the pastoral beauty of the rolling hills, the morning dew on the meadows, and the unhurried figures of the peasants behind the plows. He was among those Russian intellectuals who possessed a sense of the salubrious psychological effects of agricultural labor, "the poetics of work with the scythe in the dewy morning meadow" (Tolstoy 1965, 20:275). On June 12, 1907, Tolstoy happily claimed that "the laborer, performing the work, [is] in a more favorable position than his master, beset by the irritating news in the morning newspaper, bitterness, depression, and hemorrhoids" (ibid., 270).

Tolstoy was seeking to explain that to be happy man had to be able to separate what was important and what was not. Human life and experience were so burdened by the pursuit of ambition and pleasure, and the voice of experience so muffed by the pangs of unsatisfied desire, that only by rejecting social and material reality and following Christ's path to salvation could man acquire the kingdom of heaven. Tolstoy understood sacrifice and renunciation better than he did compromise and coexistence. The social and political environment of the times was conducive to strengthening his belief. Tolstoy knew evil; the story of his life was a long arduous road of self-mortification in an attempt to live according to his moral convictions.

Tolstoy's was a noble vision, even if it was divorced from the actual experience of the want and deprivation he and his disciples so passionately propounded.[6] The road to salvation looked to him like the epiphany of Christ's martyrdom and the altruistic deed. This is the meeting point of Tolstoy's, Berdyayev's, and Bulgakov's moral religious rhapsodizing of self-sacrifice, which was the touchstone of meaningful human work as they perceived it.

Unlike Tolstoy, whose religious temperament recoiled from work marred by human ambition and whose notion of self-sacrifice preached mortification of human desires and extolled the altruistic deed of physical work, Sergei Bulgakov's return to religion was colored by the ardent desire to impart Puritan rigor into the Russian Orthodox fervor. Bulgakov's identifying position was the infusion of a monastic religious tenor into all aspects of human activity. His was a moral and political crusade against what he perceived as the perversion of the meaning of work--the revolutionary intelligentsia's celebration of heroic deed.

Bulgakov (1871-1944),[7] the son of an Orthodox priest, entered a theological seminary, but at the age of thirteen, he experienced a religious crisis and left the seminary. At the time of his studies at Moscow University, he became an enthusiastic Marxist and specialized in political economy. He went to Western Europe to work on his thesis. In his thesis, *Capitalism and Agriculture* (1900), Bulgakov tested the basic propositions of Marxism in the field of agriculture and came to the conclusion that Marx's thesis was not justified by agricultural evolution. In coming to his position that the fundamental principles of social and individual life must be established in connection with a theory of the absolute value of goodness, truth, and beauty, Bulgakov drew upon the German idealism of Kant. In 1903, Bulgakov reflected on the profound impact of his research, which "shattered [his] faith in his ideals" (Zenkovsky 1953,2:891). Between 1901 and 1906, while he chaired the department of political economy at the Kiev Polytechnic Institute, Bulgakov underwent a second spiritual crisis--this time in a religious direction. Bulgakov renounced the doctrines of economic materialism and moved toward a religious conception of reality. In 1905, he and Berdyayev founded a journal, *Voprosy Zhizni* (*The Questions of Life*), in which they expounded their views on religious and social themes. In 1918, Bulgakov was ordained to the priesthood.

Back in 1909, in contemplating the nature of the Russian intelligentsia's penchant for heroic deed in *Heroism and Asceticism: Reflections on the Religious Nature of the Russian Intelligentsia* (1986), Bulgakov sought to dramatize what he perceived as a sharp distinction between the secular nature of a deed and the religious nature of Christian asceticism. With great passion and temper, he seemed surprisingly engaged in the mission of a Russian Calvin; for through all the bitter accusations he hurled at the revolutionaries bent on carrying out heroic deeds, we hear the violently earnest, ruggedly intractable voice of Calvin insisting on man's obedience and surrender to the will of Providence. "Christian asceticism," Bulgakov intoned,

> is unremitting self-control, struggle with the lower, sinful sides of one's character, spiritual *askesis*. True asceticism consists in faithfully fulfilling one's duty, in bearing one's own cross in self-renunciation (not just outward, but, still, more, inward) and leaving all the rest to Providence. In monastic usage there is an excellent expression for this religious and practical idea: *obedience* (Bulgakov 1986, 38-39).

Bulgakov's language echoed the Calvinist ethical maxims described by Max Weber in *The Protestant Ethic and the Spirit of Capitalism*. Bulgakov seemed to strive to endow all areas of purposeful human activity with an aura of religious authority when he suggested that "this concept [religious duty] can be extended beyond the walls of the monastery and applied to any work whatsoever" (ibid., 39). While Bulgakov, in coming to this distinction, drew on the Calvinists' "discipline of obedience" and "worldly asceticism . . . from the German expression '*innerweltliche Askese*'," and its corollaries "restraint, unflagging self-discipline, patience and endurance," his newly defined ethic of work was the product of Russian pressures. These were the pressures of self-righteous absolutism in all fields of thought and expression. With unusual insight, Bulgakov touched the nerve-center of the entire problem: the intimate connection between the Russian sense of human activity and God.

Bulgakov's identifying position--the core and, indeed, very nearly the whole of his eschatology--was the infusion of a monastic religious tenor into all aspects of human activity. Bulgakov wanted to imbed religion in the very structure of the human soul. To refute the present in order to show that future salvation is of sole importance was a curious proceeding and highly Russian. That Christian "asceticism," one of Bulgakov's favorite words, would be the source of the Russian intelligentsia's redemption, was his root principle, his position and his doctrine.

In the revolutionary intelligentsia's celebration of the heroic deed, Bulgakov jealously discerned a rival, which appropriated the religious spirit but not God:

In secular politics, the most ordinary intelligentsia maximalism, the stuff of revolutionary programs, is simply seasoned with Christian terminology or texts and served as true Christianity in politics. Like any religion, Christianity is jealous; it is strong in a person only when it seizes him entirely, soul, heart, will (ibid., 41).

Bulgakov subjected the substance of the heroic deed to radical critique to see what remained of it when God was removed from the context and man took his place. He shuddered in abhorrence at the moral picture of man without God, when "the religious cultivation of the personality" is "substituted" by "the mere communication of knowledge" (ibid., 46). Bulgakov planted himself on the ground that the Russian has a spiritual nature endowed with an equal capacity for religious sainthood, "the precepts of St. Sergei's cloister,"[8] and the destructive anarchism of "the freebooters who filled the regiments of Razin and Pugachev."[9] Therefore, Bulgakov righteously pointed out, "destruction of the age-old foundations of the people's life frees in them the dark forces which have been so numerous in Russian history" (ibid.).

Thus Bulgakov reaffirmed his mission, the mission of the salvation of the Russian people. And if his call for a "selfless quest" was almost a pastiche of the imagery of the passion of Christ, he was acutely aware of his own penchant for missionary zeal and the absolute. He admitted in the post-scriptum that even though one can hardly "approach an absolute ideal," it is, nonetheless, "obligatory" to "urge it on others, to show it to those who do not see it" (ibid., 42).

Bulgakov was the one to come up with a bold reaffirmation of the Russian's spiritual difference from Western European Christianity. And spurred by that radiant confidence in God and the Russian, he saluted the Russian soul, which "bears His [Christ's seal] on its heart" and "intensely search[es] for the City of God," in its perennial yearning for the heavenly kingdom, so "profoundly different from the bourgeois [that is Puritan Western European] desire for solid earthly well-being". He shivered in the ecstasy of revelation that "Russia, and particularly her intelligentsia," whom Fyodor Dostoyevsky compared to the "possessed man of the Gospel, who was cured by Christ alone," would be saved only by "a religious feat, invisible but mighty" (ibid., 49).

Whereas Bulgakov turned to Russian Orthodoxy to define his newly found ethic of work--Christian asceticism, Nikolai Berdyayev, in 1918, added to this argument a philosophical dimension.

Dostoyevsky showed that Russian revolutionism is a religious and metaphysical phenomenon, and not a political or social one. . . .

Revealed to him were those human thoughts and passions that already represent, not the psychology, but the ontology of human nature . . . Evil does not ultimately destroy the human image. Dostoyevsky believes that by the path of inner catastrophe evil may be transformed into good.

A German is either a mystic or a critic: a mystic at the positive pole of his thought and a critic at the negative. A Frenchman is either a dogmatist or a skeptic: a dogmatist at the positive pole of his thought and a skeptic at the negative. But a Russian is either an apocalypticist: an apocalypticist at the positive and a nihilist at the negative pole.

. . . The Russian's search for the truths of life always assumes an apocalyptic or a nihilistic attitude. This is a profound national trait. The Russian atheism has something of apocalypses, unlike the Western atheism. Russian nihilism is an inverted religion (Berdyayev 1986, 41-42).[10]

In 1909, unlike Bulgakov, who was on the threshold of his career, Nikolai Berdyayev (1874-1948) had already become one of the leading Russian philosophers of the twentieth century. Born into a military family, he received his elementary education in a military school. It might well be that the rigors of his military upbringing contributed to his lifelong deep and passionate preoccupation with the question of human freedom.

Berdyayev's spiritual evolution began with his early enthusiasm for Marxism. In his student days at Kiev University, he joined a Marxist group. He was expelled from the university, imprisoned, and then exiled. He eventually became critical of Marxism and moved to traditional Russian Orthodoxy. While Bulgakov kept cajoling his readers to move away from the heroics of social life into the ascetic rigors of Christian self-perfection, Berdyayev sought to achieve "a new consciousness" "by means of a synthesis of knowledge and faith."[11] Berdyayev, in an indomitable spirit of search for *pravda-istina* (just truth) and *pravda-spravedlivost'* (true justice), could be satisfied only by an "organic union of theory and practice." Hereupon Berdyayev, like Bulgakov, called for a return to the intrinsic Russian "intellectual tradition" of "a thirst for an integral world-view that would fuse theory and life, and a thirst for faith" (*PV*, 15).

This was a packed statement, linking in one swift series of clauses the relation of man to abstract academicism and social reality, which was permeated by his relation to a transcendent being. It is in this "demand for an integral world view of the world and of life," Berdyayev asserted, that "one can discern a streak of unconscious religiosity" (*PV*, 5).

Berdyayev's own approach to God and the search for Truth depended on "intuition" and his belief in the absolute value of "philosophical and cultural achievement." It was the Russian intelligentsia's disregard for "absolute value," Berdyayev charged, that betrays itself in "the almost insane tendency to judge philosophical doctrines and truths according to political and utilitarian criteria, and the inability to examine philosophical and cultural achievements in their essence" (*PV*, 5).

Whether his trust in philosophy hastened his rejection of Marxism one cannot surely determine. His brand of philosophy, according to V. V. Zenkovsky, was "influenced by Schopenhauer, Nietzsche, and Boehme; but he also drank deep of the basic ideas of transcendentalism" (Zenkovsky 1953, 2:762). Those foreign aids were for Berdyayev precisely aids and not the source. Berdyayev's philosophy of personal, moral redemption, the philosophy of freedom, was the logical process of the continuity of the Russian search for freedom of will.

It was a tradition rooted in the Russian philosophical views of Fyodor Dostoyevsky, Vladimir Solov'ev, and Lev Tolstoy, which acquired a distinct voice and expression in Berdyayev's suggestion that to "be freed from external oppression" and "from internal bondage" one has to "accept responsibility and cease blaming everything on external forces. Then the soul of the intelligentsia will be born" (*PV*, 16).

In mid-1918, in the wake of the destruction caused by the Bolshevik revolution and the horrors of the atrocities unleashed by the peasants in the countryside, Berdyayev in *Out of the Depths* exploded in an acrimonious assault on the Russian revolutionary intelligentsia's celebration of the revolutionary heroic deed. It was the heroic revolutionary deed, devoid of a sense of "personal moral responsibility and personal moral discipline" (*SR*, 56), which, he charged, was responsible for the calamitous effects of the Bolshevik revolution.

If Berdyayev's argument was totally rejected by both the liberal and the radical intelligentsia dedicated to political struggle and social redemption, it only underscored his argument that the Russian revolutionary intelligentsia viewed moral issues in the ethics of human activity as subordinate to the larger political and social agenda. Back in 1909, in *Signposts,* contemplating the revolutionary intelligentsia's stubborn refusal to heed his call to give up the political struggle and to start taking personal moral responsibility, Berdyayev, in an illuminating insight, prophesied: "Political liberation is possible only in conjunction with and on the basis of a spiritual and cultural renaissance" (*PV*, 15). It was an extremely bold proposition which, amidst the political and social turmoil of 1909, shifted the burden of change from outside social reality and its political institutions to the individual's personal and moral redemption.

The source of personal redemption, spiritual and cultural renaissance, Berdyayev believed, had to be sought within the Russian tradition. Berdyayev felt that the intelligentsia's "need for a philosophical sanction for its [the intelligentsia's] social aspirations" (*PV, 4*) was the culprit of its persistent perversion of Western thought. For Berdyayev, who was an astute student of Marxism and of Western European philosophical thought, noted with dismay the Russian mix of "social utilitarian" and religious fervor in adapting Western scientific positivism, which

> understood science as a special materialist dogma and the scientific spirit as a special faith: a dogma that exposed the evil of autocracy and the falsehood of the bourgeois world, and a faith that would deliver the people or the proletariat. Scientific positivism, like everything Western, was taken over in its most extreme form, and it became not only a primitive metaphysics but a special religion that replaced all earlier ones (*PV,* 8).

It was this eclectic adaptation "for domestic use" (*PV, 12*) of "dialectical materialism and neo-Kantianism" (*PV, 4*) which Berdyayev insisted constituted the revolutionary intelligentsia's perversion of Western ideas.

If Berdyayev rebelled against the Russian intelligentsia's "social utilitarianism," it was a rebellion against "the fault of the will" which "freely chose the path of worshipping man." Herein is the core and the root of Berdyayev's life credo and philosophy, the philosophy of freedom.

In 1918, pondering these fresh discoveries, Berdyayev looked back to Tolstoy to demonstrate that "Tolstoy, as a seeker of the truth of life and as a moralist and as a religious teacher, is very characteristic of Russia and the Russians" (*SR,* 55). Berdyayev's ire was leveled at "Tolstoyan individualism" which was "completely antisocial, for him there is no problem of society" (*SR,* 56). In his apostolic zeal, Berdyayev held Tolstoy responsible for "prevent[ing] the birth and development of the morally responsible individual in Russia" (*SR,* 57).

It was, according to Berdyayev, Tolstoy's interpretation of religion and, particularly, his failure to experience the "feeling of original sin the radical evil of human nature" which led him to reject "religious redemption." Herein lay the source of Tolstoy's and the Russian revolutionaries' hostility to the individual and his creative activity. For, charged Berdyayev, Tolstoy's call for a "return to a natural condition of national life, in which it sees immediate truth and goodness" became "the source of the entire philosophy of the Russian revolution" (*SR,* 59).

Berdyayev, the bard of freedom and intellectual endeavor, bitterly castigated Tolstoy for "disdainful and negative attitude toward any spiritual work and creation" and for deification "of physical labor, in which he sought salvation from the absurdity of life." Berdyayev saw a direct link between Tolstoy's "idealization" of common people and physical labor and the Russian revolution, which "raises to the heights the representatives of physical labor and degenerates representatives of spiritual labor" (*SR,* 60).

Spiritual labor and creativity were the stuff of personal freedom. Personal freedom, Berdyayev felt, was "immanent," it was subjective, and it was one's own, and this perception was the source of a true creativity. The tragedy of the Russian intelligentsia, he proposed, was its perception of "church, state, spiritual life" as an outside reality "transcendentally removed, not as immanent, its own" (*SR,* 61), and, consequently, those three categories were perceived by the intelligentsia as coercive and hostile. The reason for that anomaly, Berdyayev suggested, lay, first, in Russian monarchic rule, which excluded the Russian intelligentsia from participating in government control, and, second, in the intelligentsia's hostility toward the Russian Church which surrendered its power of authority to the Russian monarch.

Thus Berdyayev came to make the remarkable suggestion that every person carries in him a potential for redemption and that redemption is a matter of his own will, rather than of outside social reality and political institutions. The Russian could be redeemed only by intense and enduring communion with Orthodox Christianity, what Bulgakov referred to as Christian asceticism. Berdyayev therefore called for moral discipline and responsibility.

In an attempt to infuse the traditional Russian image of the passion of Christ with secular moral precepts of discipline and responsibility, Berdyayev, in the heroic deed of a religious prophet, confronted a hostile society and bared the sores of the Russian tradition. If Tolstoy, Bulgakov, and Berdyayev, in their noble mission of the salvation of the Russian people, proposed to define human work in terms of moral responsibility and Christian asceticism, it was because they, in the best of Russian tradition, believed that human work is the stuff of free will, which alone could fuse the ideal and the real and bring the heavenly kingdom on earth. Their intense belief in the redeeming force of Russian Orthodoxy revealed an ironic Russian kinship between the Christian and the revolutionary intelligentsia in their insistence on human work and was propelled by an uncompromising fierceness and passion and an unflinching allegiance to the irrational.

4

The Curse of Living:
Bunin and Chekhov

Unlike the peasant, who had an intimate experience of physical work, and Tolstoy, who insisted on appropriating this experience as the means of achieving moral perfection, some Russian writers, removed from the immediate experience of physical work, felt morally challenged by Tolstoy's philosophy, which resonated with the moral-philosophical maxims of ascetic suffering, moral perfection, and physical work. Tolstoy's voice and command were that of a philosopher and an aristocrat of comfortable means, whose philosophic proposition wished away the present and devoted itself to the perfect--self-abnegating, altruistic work in a utopian village commune of the past.

Although a philosopher could look hopefully to the past, a writer of less comfortable means, faced with the social and economic pressures of everyday life, had to deal with the ignominy of the present and the paradox of everyday life. The grand illusion of Tolstoy received powerful dramatic comments from Anton Chekhov (1869-1904) and Ivan Bunin (1870-1953), who found the narrative means to show the ironic inconsistencies between Tolstoy's philosophy and real life, between theory and practice.

Chekhov, the grandson of a serf who paid his way out of bondage, was not convinced that suffering and renunciation of mundane life were by far as salubrious to human mental health and happiness as Tolstoy had prophesied. Chekhov, who had suffered his father's beatings and lived through the pangs of abject humiliation when obliged "to kiss the hand that struck him" (Gilles 1968, 12), was deeply disturbed by the idea that suffering was the way to salvation. Chekhov explored the root of Russian preoccupation with suffering as a human weakness and of aversion to exertion, to putting up resistance to outside pressure. Chekhov's irony destroyed the illusory promise and exposed the fragility of hope. Bunin, a nobleman and an astute student of Russian village life, challenged the "benefits" of suffering and vengefully and zestfully revealed its paralyzing effect.

I call this chapter "The Curse of Living" in two senses. The first is the *curse* of being, the scourge of suffering inflicted on man in his everyday existence and his work. The second is the *curse* that symbolizes the overwhelming sense of apathy, as deep as the sense of fatalism and resignation that nurtures it. Consequently, work is recognized as an inevitable bondage and a curse. Apathy, tragic irony, resignation, and hopelessness have exposed themselves in the narrative images. To elucidate the dark paradox of the idea of suffering and its destructive effect on professional work, I find it useful to begin with Chekhov's *Palata No 6 (Ward No. 6)* of 1892.[1] This is a splendid piece of Russian prose in which Chekhov, with the unflinching eye of a surgeon, tests the image of suffering and reveals it as a deadly malaise of the Russian intelligentsia--the cause of its rationalized and, consequently, condoned inactivity, indifference, and amorality. The physical background of the story, the existing and would-be inhabitants of the lunatic asylum, ward No. 6, and their representative experiences unveil with meticulous brutality the human drama of the intellectual's grand disillusionment.

The story is propelled by the interplay of a pair of opposites: the patient in the mental asylum, Ivan Dmitrievich, and his doctor, Andrei Efimovich. The plot is thrust forward by the interaction of two conflicting philosophies of life: the cool detached rationalism of the doctor and the furious anti-rationalistic fervor of the patient. The grim paradox comes to a head in the doctor's "fall" and his fatal revelation of Truth.

The narrative develops in two frames: one is the baffling symbolism of deprivation of "Ward No. 6," and the other is the doctor's cozy six-room apartment crowded with books and magazines. First they are presented as two separate entities, as alien as their inhabitants, whose paths run parallel and never cross. The symbolism of the physical surroundings allows us to see and feel the moods and motivations permeating the scene. The way man organizes and defines the space he occupies, accepts or refuses to accept his physical surroundings yields valuable insights into the mental pictures man carries and recognizes as his own.

The story opens with a harshly explicit description of the hospital yard and the interior of its wing, ward No. 6. The spatial position of the wing, where "the front stares at the hospital and the back faces the field from which it is separated only by a grey, spiked fence" (Chekhov 1900, 131), speaks volumes about the marginality of existence in the twilight zone between civilization--the rational, the hospital--and the raw instincts of nature--the irrational, the field. The paradox then is deeply imbedded in the phenomenon of mental disease and its institutional form, Ward No. 6, which proposes to safeguard the rest of society from those who are teetering precariously between two realities, artificial [human] and natural.

The underlying rhythm of chilling despair and brutality rises to a crescendo when the reader is led from the hospital yard inward. The picture of the hospital yard, "overgrown with burdocks, nettles, and wild hemp," is succeeded by the cheerless vista of "mountains of rotting hospital trash heaped in the hallway and exuding a suffocating stench" (ibid.). The sense of a no-man's zone is evoked by the stolid, impressive bulk of the old soldier, prostrated leisurely on top of the stinking heap. The barred windows and the "foul smells of the sour cabbage, roaches and ammonia" are reminiscent of the "menagerie" (ibid., 132) and signal rupture with the human world. The metaphor of "menagerie" enhances the jarring paradox between expected specter of "caged beasts" and the actual inhabitants of the wing: a childishly gay and lively idiot, Moiseika, who loves to help his wretched companions, and the perennially agitated Ivan Dmitrievich, who, since his initial introduction, takes center stage and acquires the metaphoric symbolism of ward No. 6.

Aged thirty-three and of noble birth, Ivan Dmitrievich suffers from persecution mania. Chekhov injects his personal feeling of attachment to Ivan Dmitrievich's "attractive face, lined with the traces of suffering and eternal terror" (ibid., 134). In the evenings Ivan Dmitrievich erupts in incoherent speeches, vitriolic jibes against "human baseness, violence tramping over truth," he speaks about the "beauty of the future life, and of the barred windows, which ever remind him of the stupidity and cruelty of the strong" (ibid., 135). Born into a very wealthy family, Ivan Dmitrievich studied at St. Petersburg University, but fifteen years prior to his present confinement his father was imprisoned for alleged embezzlement and died in disgrace. Ivan Dmitrievich had to give up his studies and support himself. Unable to sustain any friendship because of his irritable and suspicious nature, he is miserably lonely. He despises his fellow citizens for their gross ignorance and torpid base life. He passionately laments the absence of meaningful life and spiritual interests. He rages at the dullness of a life punctuated by violence, coarse debauchery, and hypocrisy, a life where honest men are starving, while crooks feast in luxury. He bemoans the town's indigence, which "cries out for schools, honest newspapers, a unity of intellectual forces" (ibid., 136). For Ivan Dmitrievich, as for Lev Tolstoy, the writer, humankind is split into absolute good and absolute evil, "the honest men and the scoundrels with nothing in between" (ibid.). Ivan Dmitrievich was jolted into his first fit of manic fear by the sight of two convicts in chains. In a split second, he realized that he could have been in the place of those convicts, even though he would never kill or harm anyone.

> Folk wisdom teaches the person that poverty or imprisonment can strike anyone. A mistake in the judicial system is very possible, given the present system of legal proceedings. People who treat the suffering of others in a business-like, official manner, as do judges, policemen, doctors, in the course of time, as the result of habit, lose their sensitivity to such a degree that they cannot, even if they want to, treat their clients other than formally. In this respect, they are hardly different from the peasant who is unaware of the blood when he slaughters sheep and calves in his backyard. Given the formal, inhuman relation to the personality, it is only the matter of time before the innocent person is stripped of all his possessions and sent to the gallows as the result of a judicial mistake (ibid., 138).

The more Ivan Dmitrievich mulls over the social system, the more he becomes convinced that it is ridiculous to expect justice "when society regards violence in any form as rational, expedient and necessary, when any act of mercy, like the 'no guilty' verdict, causes eruption of unallayed vengeance" (ibid.). His spiritual torture, which is inflamed and aggravated by his futile attempts to be consistent and reasonable, overwhelms him. Unable to resist the tormenting fears, he surrenders to terror and despair.

His first encounter with the doctor, Andrei Efimovich, who had been invited to tend him represents the travesty of his dark premonitions about the heartless indifference of the professional. The doctor announces that it would not be right "to prevent Ivan Dmitrievich from losing his mind" (ibid., 141). Eventually Ivan Dmitrievich is placed in ward No. 6.

Andrei Efimovich's accidental venture into the hospital wing signals an entirely new stage in the narration. It is the imminent collision of two perceptions, the Tolstoyan, rational philosophy of the doctor, with the Chekhovian irrational philosophy of the mental patient. The setting of the meeting reveals the deep undercurrents of sporadic human spells of compassion and persistent professional indifference. When the doctor shows his friend out, he is accidentally confronted by the inmate Moiseika, who is on his way to the ward. Seeing the wretched creature, shivering with cold, hatless, his bare feet thrust in rubbers, the doctor, with mixed feelings of pity and disgust, follows him into the ward. Inside, he is barraged by Ivan Dmitrievich, who accuses the doctor of incompetence for keeping him, Ivan Dmitrievich, locked up while hundreds of mentally sick are out free. Ivan Dmitrievich asks, "You, your assistant, all those scoundrels in your hospital personnel, are morally worse than we are. Why, then, are we locked up and not you? Where's the logic?"(ibid., 159). To this the doctor responds, "Morality and logic have nothing to do with it. Everything is a matter of chance. Who was caught is locked up, who was not caught is free, that's all. The fact that I am a doctor and you are a mental patient is neither a matter of morality nor logic, it is a pure accident" (ibid.). Ironically, the doctor confirms the very fears that have caused Ivan Dmitrievich's mental breakdown.

The vibrations of the paradoxical connection between Ivan Dmitrievich's feverish phobia of arbitrary jurisdiction and the doctor's detached acknowledgement of its actuality reveal the dilemma of human work in the hostile environment. The clashing perceptions of Ivan Dmitrievich, who actually experiences physical deprivation, and the doctor, who intellectually exalts physical suffering, reveals with admirable succinctness Chekhov's biting counterattack on the Tolstoyan celebration of suffering and surrender. The matchless cadence of the doctor's panegyric to suffering, which is almost an exact pastiche of Tolstoy's, illuminates the convulsive conflict that is the harbinger of imminent tragedy.

Buoyed up by a belief in the supreme value of the human intellect, the doctor proposes that Ivan Dmitrievich's lack of physical freedom does not prevent him from being happy because the sense of happiness is derived from the intellect, which transcends and "scorns the silly life vanities" (ibid., 162). The intellect and the scorn for real life, the doctor insists, "are the two blessings. . . . You, too, can possess them even if you live behind three bars. Diogenes lived in a barrel and was happier than the kings" (ibid.).

Behind the doctor's exaltation of suffering, one hears the ripples of Chekhov's derisive laughter, mocking rationality undefiled by experience. The doctor's self-righteous, brutally utilitarian rationalization of suffering is exposed by Ivan Dmitrievich as fraudulent and shallow and as drained of the actual experience of physical abuse and deprivation. Ivan Dmitrievich reveals the dulling inhumanness of celebrated suffering, because in real life "people react to suffering with tears, cries, indignation or revulsion. The lower the organism, the less intense is its reaction to irritation, the higher the organism, the more sensitive and energetic is its reaction to reality" (ibid., 166).

It is the mental patient, who, with marvelous insight and clarity, taps the root of the doctor's scientific rationality. He scrupulously peels off one vice after another to reveal, lurking behind the intellectual pomp, an indolent, weak personality whose resignation of his professional duties makes him a willing accomplice and an immediate executor of social injustice.

> The stoics, whom you travesty, were outstanding people. Their theory fossilized two thousand years ago and has not moved an inch since then. It won't move because it is unpractical and unrealistic. This theory was a success with a tiny minority who spent their lives studying and relishing it; the majority, however, did not understand it. For the majority who never knew wealth or life's pleasures and whom you scorn for suffering scorns their own lives made up of the feelings of hunger, cold, loss, insult, and a Hamletian terror of death. Those feelings are life. You can hate those feelings, but you can't scorn them (ibid., 167).

Ivan Dmitrievich's explicit reference to Jesus Christ, who "reacted to reality with tears, smiles, sadness, anger, and even anguish. . . . [Who] did not smile at his sufferings, nor did he scorn death, but prayed to escape this terrible lot" (ibid., 168), shifts the corollary about the nature of suffering into a new domain where physical rather than intellectual, suffering is part of man's experience. The doctor, who slurs over the physical depravity of his patients has never experienced physical abuse; therefore, he can stare placidly at the rampant, physical abuse around him and wave it off as another of life's paradoxes. Ivan Dmitrievich indicts the doctor's (and the Tolstoyan) rationalization of the utility of suffering as a "convenient philosophy that erases any difference between the doctor's comfortable study and the rancid mental ward, divests the person from any moral responsibility" (ibid., 169).

In another jab at Tolstoy's call for surrender and renunciation of science and modernization, Chekhov extends himself to explore different facets of the doctor's work practices. Unable to reconcile the wonders of modern medical science with the inevitability of death and misery, the doctor compares a mental hospital in Vienna where patients enjoy humane treatment with the sordid ward No. 6. The doctor lulls his pangs of conscience with the comfortable conclusion that no scientific discovery can improve life and faults the evil system for his neglect of his professional duties.

Whether there is antiseptic and Koch and Pasteur, the reality has not changed. People are still sick, and they still die. They entertain the mentally sick with balls and performances, but they do not let them out. Therefore, all is sheer vanity, and there is no difference between the Viennese clinic and mine. The position I serve is evil; I get paid by the people whom I cheat; I am dishonest. But I am only a small element in a larger system of imperative social evil. All provincial officials are evil and do not work for their pay. . . . Therefore, I am not guilty of dishonesty; it is the historical period. . . . Had I been born two hundred years later, I would have been different (ibid., 156).

Chekhov's revenge is subtle and profound. In an ironic twist, the doctor's joy in his conversations with the mental patient becomes the cause of his loss of freedom, of his shift into becoming a mental patient himself. The hospital officials, prodded by a young ambitious doctor who covets Andrei Efimovich's position, first remove the doctor from his post. Paradoxically, the doctor becomes a victim of the professional negligence he consciously perpetuated as a doctor. He is locked up in ward No. 6. The matchless description of philosophical doctrine tested in the harsh reality of the mental ward erupts in a bitter ire that overwhelms the doctor and strips away his freedom and his comfortable study, all of which he had previously insisted was irrelevant to him. For the first time in his life, he experiences, rather than rationalizes, the terror of despair.

In a pattern coterminous with Tolstoy's, Chekhov makes the pangs of suffering the ultimate revelation of the real meaning of life. Locked up as a beast of prey, the doctor rages at the social structure that leaves "a smart, educated, proud, freedom-loving person, created in God's image, the only option of being a god-damned physician in a dirty, silly provincial town" (ibid., 191). Looking back at his own life, however, he is forced to admit his own weakness and inability to withstand pressure and says, "We are weak, we are rotten" (ibid., 192). In the agonizing moment of revelation, when he is brutally beaten by the warden and experiences, for the first time in his life, the terror of physical pain, a flash of knowledge dawns upon him--the hell of suffering his patients were subjected to over the twenty years he was in charge. "He did not know, therefore he was not guilty. But his conscience as rude and vicious as the warden's fists sent an icy thrill through his body" (ibid., 194-95). The doctor dies from an apoplectic stroke.

The doctor, who was as distrustful as Tolstoy of the future and its promise of immortality, in his death is deprived of honor and promise.

Chekhov's intentional juxtaposition of the sublime, "a herd of deers of unsurpassing beauty and grace raced by," with the mundane, "a peasant woman handed him a registered letter" (ibid., 196), degrades the noble, which he coveted, and mockingly leaves him with the mundane, which he scorned and avoided all his life.

Chekhov's absorption with physical suffering was tinged with the ever-present awareness of his own illness. Back in 1884, when he was starting his own medical career, he was diagnosed with tuberculosis, which would cast a long and painful shadow on his life and work. He died of it in 1904, at the age of forty-four. His intimate knowledge of suffering and disease underlies his sense that mental sickness represents an outgrowth of a social, rather than a neurological, disorder. Ivan Dmitrievich's despairing soliloquy in which he cries, "Oh God, is it possible that there is no hell and the scoundrels will be forgiven? Where is justice?" (ibid., 194), gives voice to Chekhov's own preoccupation with the question of suffering caused by the evil social structure. Chekhov's evil is especially ominous and depressing because it is insidious and permeates the whole society beyond the mental ward. Chekhov's evil is stripped of any dramatic overtones. It is omnipresent; it oozes from the indifference and snobbishness of the townspeople who believe that the abomination of the hospital is well suited for the poor and who know no better and from the doctor's conscious neglect of his professional duties.

Chekhov's ache was more psychological than physical, for he sensed the ultimate irony that locked up in the mental asylum both the believer in future salvation, Ivan Dmitrievich, and the one who resigned all hope, the doctor. Having refuted both salvation and surrender, Chekhov is left with a gnawing sense of profound sadness and melancholic despair in the face of the ignominious present. This is part of the Russian theme.

The world of the mental ward, torpid and benumbing in its indifference, sparks with life and furious humanity only when Ivan Dmitrievich, the supposed mental patient, appears on the scene. His brutally revealing soliloquies light up with the passionate, if short-lived, fury of a firecracker the tragic symbolic images of the cursed present.

If Chekhov censored Tolstoy for his preoccupation with surrender and the past, he nonetheless bore no illusions about the present and the future. The order-worshipping warden, who mercilessly beat the patients, symbolizes the inhumanity of bureaucratic society which values order above humanity.

As we leave the cheerless cemetery where Chekhov buried Andrei Efimovich's and the Tolstoyan ideal of "renunciation and surrender," we move into the backwoods of provincial Russia in Ivan Bunin's masterful

novel *Derevnia (The Village)* written in 1909-1910.[2] Bunin's deep distaste for the village way of life and for villagers is revealed in the
opening scene which describes a highway leading to a town trade fair.
As early as the first paragraph, the tableau of the people and the
elements "the weather brightened up, the wind died down" (Bunin 1934,
7), accord the narrative, the sense of hope that resides in the town as
opposed to the village. The promise of hope is voiced in the string of
eloquent metaphors describing the town: "the light and shade stretch
along the yard, which seems beautiful, . . . and even magic. What
warmth, it can be found only in the town! . . . the night is gay and
festive" (ibid., 9).

The mood of hope, however, is frustrated by an abrupt switch in the
narration from the poetics of the night fair to the chilling family history
of the Krasovs, whose serf grandfather was hunted down by the prince's
borzois.[3] The change of mood from the festivity and jocularity of the
town to the gloominess and morbidity of the village is punctuated by the
somber notes of violent death and casts a deep shadow of doubt over the
sense of hope. Moreover, the narrative's constant shuttle between the village and the provincial town bridges the gap between both and reveals
their deeply imbedded similarities.

The narration is centered on one of the Krasovs, Tikhon, who is now
the owner of the estate where his grandfather met his death. Tikhon is
the richest self-made merchant in his village. His road to riches from
peddler to owner of a coaching inn and pub, and later to wheat and land
trader, is deprived of a sense of victory and achievement.

The entire rhythm of Tikhon's work, which is filled with cows, hogs,
horses, and sheep and keeps him tied hand and foot to his vast holdings,
is thrown off track by the nagging insidious thought that the fruit of his
ambition is deceptive wealth, which has turned his life into "a gaol"
(ibid., 22, 24). As if to emphasize the senselessness of the frenzy of
work and to strip him of any dignity and pride, Tikhon is bereft of
children and the sense of purpose and continuity associated with them.
Tikhon's inability to have children represents the vibrations of his ebbing
sense of hope and the fruitlessness of his ambition. It bears testimony to
the spiritual unity between Bunin and Tolstoy, who warned that hard
work to satisfy one's ambition would bring misery and unhappiness.

If Bunin acknowledged the misery of ambition, he was ambivalent
about the way out. Bunin felt, as did Chekhov, that individual life was
a constant confrontation between a person and the larger society. But
Bunin came closer than Chekhov did to reflecting on the circular nature
of mutual dependency between the individual and the social structure.
For Tikhon's "cross"--his wealth, his numerous cows, sheep, and hogs,

and his land holdings--that turned his life into a bondage, directly
addresses this condition of dependency. The metaphor of wealth "that
holds him in tight clutches" (ibid., 69) evokes the feeling of a victim
harassed by a pitiless enemy. What we have here then, is the sense of
alienation between a person and his achievement, between a person and
the fruit of his ambition.

Bunin felt, as did Chekhov, that death was the only path to salvation.
Unlike Tolstoy, Bunin believed that man could transcend the curse of
living in no way other than death. It is the ultimate promise of peace and
ultimate salvation which takes on symbolic meaning in Tikhon's tortuous
attempts to come to terms with the burden of his wealth. The symbolic
image of death as a viable alternative to senseless life and work is
resurrected in the very beginning and the very end of the novel. It is in
the tranquility of a cemetery that Tikhon manages to shake off the feeling
of bile and anguish which overcame him at the sight of pervasive poverty
and degradation at the town trade fair. The metaphor of "the peace and
sunbathed serenity of the churchyard cemetery" (ibid., 28), which erases
the difference between "the pauper and the tsar" (ibid., 30), questions
and belittles the validity of earthly ambitions. The magnetism of Bunin's
cemetery, its air of stability and security among the fragility and
instability of human life ironically defies any hope for happiness, not
only in the present, but also in the future.

The sentiment is paradoxically confirmed and enlarged in the closing
chapter of the novel, when Tikhon is on the verge of a drastic move
from the village into the town. In a telling twist, it is not the move that
gives Tikhon a sense of happiness, but a passage from the Bible, which
declares earthly activity sterile and vacuous "human vanity" and human
life "a dream and dreaming" (ibid., 179).

If social life has no hope in the village, nor in the provincial town, it
manifests Bunin's skepticism of possible social change. Bunin's sardonic
laughter punctuates the scene of a mocking desecration of authority and
law by a tipsy cossack who first exposes himself and then hacks and
wounds passersby. Set against circulating rumors of impending
parliamentarism and constitutional rights, the scene challenges and vio-
lates the sense of promise and impending change.

Bunin scoffed at Tolstoy's attempts to represent the Russian past as a
viable alternative to the existing evil. Bunin lashed out at the way of life
which made the cursed present possible. It was the inevitable outcome,
he believed, of the circular movement between people who condone
violence and surrender to it and political institutions which perpetrate
this violence. "Pushkin[4] was killed, Lermontov[5] was murdered, Pisarev[6]
was drowned, Ryleev[7] was hanged, Dostoyevsky was dragged to execu-

tion. . . . You say the government is to blame?   All people get the government they deserve" (ibid., 95).

Bunin's sense of bafflement and despair rips the scene of provincial Russia, where nature's bounty is rendered meaningless by animal-like hopelessness, and wretched human existence.

What wealth! Black earth, almost blue, fat, lush greenery of the trees, gardens. . . . But the huts--made of clay, tiny, covered with dung-roof. . . . Herein is a rich house . . . but there is dirt knee-deep everywhere, and a pig is sprawled on the porch. The windows are tiny, the inside is dark, overcrowded with things and people; the sleeping benches, a huge stove, a bucket with slops . . . everyone hates everyone and they wish the other to "to choke on his piece of bread on the holiday"; the grandmother, swinging her dark sinewy hands, screams her heart out at the daughters-in-law, spurts spittle and curses either one or the other, . . . the angry sick grandfather wears everybody down with his moralizing (ibid., 113).

With masterly strokes which betray a native love of extremes, Bunin plunges the reader from the suffocating, hellish despair of the interior into the senseless boisterousness of the dancing muzhiks, who are cheered by a crowd of their peers. The jaunting juxtaposition of misery and the feast, which is analogous to a feast in the midst of a plague, adds to the complex feeling of revulsion, sympathy, and ironic mockery.

In the scene of a stuck carriage whose helpless victims, escaping a fire set to their estate by the peasants, are mocked and taunted by sneering muzhiks (ibid, 117), the tenuous, fragile peace is seen as teetering on the edge of violent explosion. A deadly threat lurks in the sardonic smile and blood-freezing stare of a garden warden, Akim, who burns with desire to kill and destroy everything, even the nightingale.

Bunin's revulsion for the bloodthirsty and deceptively pious peasants and his ambivalent mix of sympathy and vexation toward the hard-nosed and hardworking Tikhon, become skeptically cordial when Tikhon's brother Kuz'ma steps into the narration. An obvious antipode of Tikhon, Kuz'ma revels in studying, writing, and passive contemplation. His ambition is to "tell about his doomed life, to expose unflinchingly his poverty and the maiming experience of everyday existence, which has deprived him of all hope" (ibid., 92).

Kuz'ma's valiant attempts to transcend the pain of everyday life and the biting travesty of Tolstoy's teaching reveal Bunin's own skepticism toward work as a viable source of happiness. It might well be that we hear in this episode the echo of Bunin's own disappointing attempts at adhering to Tolstoy's ideas of moral perfection and manual work.[8] When Kuz'ma heeds Tolstoy's call for the poor, his impression of the simple and honest life of physical work is ripped apart by the brutality of the Russian village, which is the aberration of the idyllic Tolstoyan patriarchal abode. The wretchedness of village life unrelentingly detailed in Kuz'ma's utopian attempts to become a hard-working agricultural laborer represents Bunin's sardonic refraction of the Tolstoyan celebration of material poverty and salubrious agricultural labor.

Bunin, as well as Chekhov, bore no illusions about the viability of the Tolstoyan belief in purposeful human work. The chiaroscuro of Kuz'ma's unsuccessful attempts to find any employment to save himself from starvation and his gradual moral and physical degradation and the eloquent vignettes describing the larger social degradation give voice to Bunin's mockery of salvation.

Having brought Kuz'ma to the end of his tether, to a point where he must choose between retreating to a monastery or committing suicide, Bunin feels compelled to test his hero in an illusory paradise where his desire for creative work would get its chance for fulfillment. The reprieve is, however, fraught with bitter disappointments that are forewarned by the figure of a fool who, paradoxically, is given the noble task of the messenger of hope. The silly name and attire of Motia the Duckhead, a tipsy, flour-dusted figure who wears a straw hat badly battered by cart wheels, ridicules the promise of hope, for it is he who hands the desperate Kuz'ma an invitation from his brother Tikhon to take over the management of his estate.

The paradox of "paradise found" comes to a head in the brutally revealing description of Kuz'ma's physical degeneration, which is succinctly summarized by the phrase "half-bestial existence" (ibid., 157). Despite ample opportunity to write and work, Kuz'ma spends his days aimlessly wandering about the estate, bitterly castigating himself for his lack of will, for conveniently "waiting for the lucky days to work" (ibid., 151). There is a striking similarity between Chekhov's Andrei Efimovich, an intellectual, and Bunin's Kuz'ma, a semiliterate townsman. Behind Kuz'ma's dream of "living as fate would have it, as long as it provides him with a piece of bread, and of course, under his brother's protection" (ibid., 169) is Bunin's acknowledgment that his hero lacks the desire or will to fend for himself and surrenders his life to destiny and the mercy of his brother. Although Kuz'ma grows to identify himself with the villagers and the dulling torpor of their daily routine, his ambitious and industrious brother Tikhon feels revolted by the same things that paralyze and mesmerize Kuz'ma.

If Bunin dispatches Tikhon and Kuz'ma out of the village, if he brings the weak-willed, partially educated Kuz'ma into the custody of the tough, avaricious, uneducated Tikhon, it makes only too salient Bunin's unambiguous distrust of the educated and intellectually ambitious who were short on action. Kuz'ma's will, reduced to a shadow of his brother's, manifests Bunin's belief that the promise of change does not lie in intellectual power. However, Tikhon's raw power of greed and acquisition gets no reprieve either. Neither Kuz'ma's utopianism nor Tikhon's utilitarianism are allowed to escape the daunting realization that their everyday life is a waste, "human vanity, dream and dreaming" (ibid., 179).

Bunin was convinced that a large part of the blame for existing misery and poverty lay in the inherent inability of the Russian to pursue his ambition with vigor, dedication, and persistence. In the ultimate paradox, Bunin's and Chekhov's recognition that human work offers no salvation echoed Tolstoy's warning against work as the means to satisfy one's ambition. If their voices are full of prophetic sternness, melancholy, and despair, that is because they sought perfection and wholesomeness in the inherently unwholesome social reality. Unable to reconcile the ideal with the real, they retreated and surrendered to despair.

5

Apotheosis of Heroic Deed: Andreev and Gorky

> In your death you'll acquire immortality.
>
> Leonod Andreev, *To the Stars*

Leaving the receding, lulling rhythms of subdued sufferings and quelled expectations behind, we move away from Bunin's village and Chekhov's provincial town into a world where suffering erupts in open defiance to the ignominy of living. Hope takes center stage, and the voice of suffering carries the promise of salvation.

If salvation were to come, it would come through self sacrifice and death. Any attempt to circumvent direct confrontation, to cushion the clash, to modify the existing structure was vehemently condemned as reactionary. The implacable tones of the confrontation between those who sought to modify existing conditions and those who demanded their complete and total destruction were enunciated in the vitriolic jibes against hard work as inherently exploitative. The Marxist revolutionary idea of active participation in political life reverberated in the growing numbers of underground social democratic circles and rose to a crescendo assault upon the socioeconomic and political institutions. In 1902, an anonymous contributor to the social democratic emigre journal *Zhizn'* *(Life)* spouted indignation and contempt for the exploitative nature of productive labor.

> The peasant who grows rich works equally hard alongside the laborers he has hired in times of crisis. They are, literally, worn down, due to

the nature of agricultural work and the owner. The latter works at heightened speed to coerce the laborers in an inhuman effort to sustain his tempo.

Whether one wants or not, one is forced to compare this system to the sweatshop system, which everybody recognizes as exploitative (1902, 6:298).

Behind righteous indignation against the harsh reality of survival, one clearly discerns the Russian prejudice against the slavish nature of agricultural work. A salvo of metaphors painstakingly catalogs the misery of summer fieldwork, the pangs of physical suffering in "the blistering summer heat," and the "scorching sun rays" (ibid., 301). The censoring tone and the insidious image of the unholy unity of suffering and labor effectively humbles and diminishes the link between labor and salvation.

The Russian revolutionary's fascination with Marxism reveals the point of convergence between Russian culture and Marxist ideas. Marx's attack on rapacious capitalism sounded a responsive chord in the Russian's ire against the injustices of the system. Marx's promise of a proletarian revolution and a perfect society resonated in the Russian's belief in ultimate justice and universal salvation.

Russian revolutionary thinking, however, was the product of native pressures. It imbued Marxism with the Russian religious value of the passion of Christ. Salvation, it was commonly felt, was inextricably associated with ascetic life and self-sacrifice in the course of violent political struggle. According to both the religious and secular proponents of this belief, the loftiness of the aim fully justified the means. The Russian revolutionary's belief in active participation in political life found its voice and authority in V. D. Bonch-Bruevich's articles on the Russian schism[1] which were published in *Zhizn'*. It is instructive to observe the irony of his fusion of the secular and the religious. In his articles, Bonch-Bruevich, a revolutionary, cites a religious believer as a voice of authority on the sanctity of revolutionary violence. Bonch-Bruevich, who in 1903 headed the branch of Russian social democrats in Geneva and was responsible for forwarding the illegal literature of the Bolshevik party into Russia, felt, as did the religious believer he cites in one of his articles, that revolutionary destruction was beneficial. Notably, it is this religious believer who injects the religious ethos of the passion of Christ into human activity. Behind the fervent rationalization of violence and call for self-sacrifice, one hears a passionate belief in the necessity of redefining human activity.

Riots, plunder, and devastation are to be looked upon as evil if they are committed by villains for their cruel, mercenary ends; if, however, people commit acts of violence not for their own ends, but for the ben-enefit of the whole Russian people, you can no longer call those acts "riots," "plunder," and "devastation." Whether it is good or bad to de-stroy the churches or break the icons, all that depends on the circum-stances (Bonch-Bruevich 1902, 6:264-65).

What we hear is the insistence on differentiation between activities. The activity which leads to salvation is required to adopt a new name; it is undefiled by the evil present. The sense of analogy between the intensity of human belief and the human action which manifests this belief receives its ultimate expression in the act of martyrdom for the sake of mankind and is voiced, according to Bonch-Bruevich, by the same religious believer.

We believe that love can be measured only with self-sacrifice, for there is no greater love than the one that leads a person to give his life for his friends. We think, therefore, that the revolutionary who resorts to violence and gives his life for his friends is closer to Christ than the one who babbles about surrender (ibid., 265).

Inasmuch as the report comes indirectly through a person who propounded and worked diligently for the revolution, it seems to reflect the genuine mood of a certain segment of the Russian schismatics.[2] This report voiced a push from the muted lamentation of suffering to the vigorous pathos of heroic self-sacrifice. The push was enunciated and given the power of representation in the play *K Zvezdam (To the Stars)*. Written by Leonid Andreev (1871-1919) in 1906, the play speaks of the writer's search for meaning of human activity when the euphoria after the short-lived Russian revolution of 1905 began to subside.

Here, I explore the perception in the Russian literature of the heroic deed as the only valid and moral human work. Unlike Tolstoy, who yearned for a mythical patriarchal past, and Chekhov and Bunin, who despaired of any hope, Andreev and Gorky looked to the future, to a future cleansed of the evils of the present. A shift in the setting, a movement away from the province, marked a shift in the mood, which was tense with the confrontation between the proponents of surrender and the advocates of revolutionary salvation.

Ironically, Andreev intended to write his first play, which turned out to be the only one of his plays in which revolutionary activities were given prominence, in collaboration with Gorky. Andreev wrote it, however, on his own, as Gorky was imprisoned at the time for his revolutionary activity. But it was Gorky who became a powerful mouthpiece of impending revolutionary salvation and its heroic deeds.

Leonid Andreev grasped in the confrontation between the proponents of surrender and of revolutionary salvation the Russian ambivalence to work, which was enunciated in the ambiguous, if subtle, ethnic differentiation between surrender and the heroic deed. Surrender, an escape from reality into intellectual endeavor, erects a high wall between the individual and the rest of the society. Its ultimate representation is total isolation and self-imposed loneliness. Heroic deed, however, carries the promise of hope. Heroism means active participation in political activities. It defies the accepted, preaches, leads, suffers, and brings, in death, the promise of redemption.

If Andreev's celebration of death, the epitome of self-sacrifice, muddles scientific endeavor and the heroic deed, it is because he, like Tolstoy, yearned for perfection, which transcended the boundaries of human life. Cosmic space and its promise of eternity celebrate both heroic self-sacrifice and intellectual endeavor.

Unlike Andreev's, Gorky's notion of work was undefiled by doubts and preferences. For Gorky, the meaning of man's life and work was defined by his impact on the crowd, by his power to lead it to redemption. The tone and rhythm of the passion of Christ lends newly defined fervor and passion to the human drama of growing self-awareness and the shaping of a revolutionary martyr. This was the realm explored by Gorky.

I begin with Andreev because he exhibits an ironic conflict which reveals a love of the extreme and an intolerance of anything that is less than whole. In the course of this conflict, the meaning of work acquires the symbolism of the noble, if in practice unviable, notion of self-sacrifice.

The setting of Andreev's play, an observatory cut off from the rest of the world, introduces his dramatic vision of the Russian intellectual and his work. The observatory, high in the mountains, closer to the stars than to human habitat, is a twilight zone between nature and civilization, between the eternal and the transient. The sense of the cosmic irrelevance of space and time is accentuated by the visible absence of geographical names and chronological data. The ambiguous location, which hints of some European country, underscores the sense of universalism of science and revolutionary work. But despite the claim for universalism, the conflict between the director of the observatory, Professor Ternovskii, and his children, who are actively involved in some unspecified revolutionary activities in some unspecified localities, is palpable, and it is Russian.

The degree of actual tension reflects the degree of Andreev's divided sympathies toward the contending parties. But there is more to the Russian element than meets the eye. The invocation of monasticism and the first Christians, explicit in the description of the austere furnishings and sparse decorations, becomes a full-blown metaphor when the picture of the Magi, brought by the star to Jesus, is placed among the portraits of the astronomers. Within the context of the picture of the Magi among the pictures of astronomers, Ternovskii's own work as an astronomer overshadows and obliterates his family and other worldly concerns and symbolizes the promise of redemption. For Ternovskii, an astronomer, then, is transformed into one of the Magi in the picture. The inferred link between stars, the subject of astronomy, and Jesus affirms Ternovskii's belief that the celestial is more important than the mundane. The rhythm and the pitch for the conflict is set.

The professor's descendence onto the stage is heavily loaded with the sense of suffering and loss. Some moments before his entrance, badly shaken revolutionaries, whose insurrection was brutally suppressed, bring news that Nikolai, one of the professor's sons, has probably been killed. The sense of loss challenges the celestial indifference of scientific endeavor. The astronomer's innocent question from above the staircase, "Do they still kill? Are there prisons still?" (Andreev, in *P'esy* 1959, 42) is punctuated by the emphatically malicious observation by one of the revolutionaries that "he's fallen from the moon [literally, from the sky]" (ibid.).

From hereon the conflict is pervasive; it is enlarged in the poignant symbolism of the stars. The stars, ironically, symbolize consummate intellectual endeavor, which demands that the scientist renounce all human ties and transcend human life and its miseries. It is not an intentional paradox, but Andreev's fluctuating allegiance to intellectual endeavor and its requirement for wholeness makes him anthropomorphize the stars and make them silent accomplices in the execution of a revolutionary. The metaphor of the stars, which are accorded faces, in combination with the face of the executioner, the only "faces their condemned comrade was permitted to see before his death" (ibid., 66), illuminates the insidious analogy with the astronomer. Although indirect, the sense of hostility is, nonetheless, tangible and acute.

But the analogy is even more palpable and incriminating in the crazed gory visions of the stars, the metaphors for science and man's absolute devotion to it, that Lunts, one of Ternovskii's assistants, has. Lunts's sense of guilt because his devotion to astronomy kept him away from saving his parents, who were massacred in a pogrom, brings him to the brink of a nervous breakdown. The intensity of the conflict and the explosive nature of its irreconcilable extremes reflects Andreev's craving for the absolute in good and evil.

From this vantage point, Andreev's play can be read as an endorsement of wholesomeness. The metaphor of the stars acquires the meaning of the promise of salvation and is a masterful refraction of the symbolic imagery of the opening scene (the picture of the Magi and Jesus). What is important about the stars to the professor, and to Andreev, is the message they bring of eternity and the universality of life, which transcend human preoccupation with daily misery and the fear of death. "For human intellect is as free as a bird, a powerful and free queen of space. Man himself tied up her wings and put her in cage" (ibid., 77). The metaphor of a bird as human intellect alludes to the idea of free will, and Andreev's deep preoccupation with the question of human work in the inherently constrictive social reality.

Like Tolstoy, Andreev sought the meaning of human work in the symbolic imagery of the passion of Christ. However, Andreev's belief in self-sacrifice tended to vacillate between his allegiance to scientific endeavor and the revolutionary deed. Despite his doubts, he seemed quite firm in his conviction that man was only an appendage to the lofty task of universal salvation.

The professor's rhetorical question, "how then can I cry over one soul!" (ibid., 77) depersonalizes the victim and alleviates the tragedy of human loss. It shifts the accent from the individual plane to the universal realm of salvation. The closing conversation between the astronomer and Nikolai's bride, Marusia, brings out with intense clarity Andreev's passionate plea for self-effacing human involvement, whether it is cosmic intellectual endeavor or revolutionary work.

Marusia: "Father, I can not leave the earth, I do not want to leave it, it is so miserable. It breathes terror and anguish--but I was born by it, in my blood I carry its suffering. The stars are alien to me, I do not know who lives there . . . .As a wounded bird, my soul keeps falling on the ground. . . . I will go on with the revolutionary work."
Ternovskii: "Go! Give yourself to it. . . . You'll die, as did Nikolai, as do all those whose souls, immensely happy, will sustain the eternal light. In your death you will acquire immortality. To the stars!" (ibid., 87)

And flowing from the astronomer's statement, there is another proposition being tested and amplified in the explicit glorification of self-sacrifice--the insignificance of individual life. Measured against the universe, the significance of the human as an individual is dwarfed and eliminated. The universal invalidates the mundane and celebrates the heroic deed, which challenges and defies it.

If Andreev vacillated between intellectual endeavor and revolutionary deed, Maxim Gorky, his mentor and a longtime friend, seemed at a first glance to be free of doubts. There is a subtle irony in the fact that Gorky, whose name was originally Peshkov, but who adopted a pen-name that symbolized suffering--Gorky means "bitter" in Russian--would fourteen years later condemn the Russian preoccupation with suffering as self-destructive. The shift in his ideas had to do, I believe, with Gorky's close association with the Russian social democrats and their Marxist ideas of active participation in the social process. Insofar as Gorky filtered their theories through his own prism of experience, it was this idea of active involvement, which, it seems to me, propelled Gorky on his ideological quest for an apostolic route to salvation. Gorky eventually penetrated beyond suffering and despair to the radiant brilliance of a new spirit of work which would eradicate both suffering and despair.

If ever there was a fictional savior who was unambiguously treated and celebrated for his heroic deed of altruistic self-sacrifice, it was the hero of Gorky's *Mat' (Mother)* (1907),[3] a defiant figure of redemption set against the inimical authority. The transfiguration of a working person into a revolutionary leader, a secularized Christian martyr, was invested by Gorky with the passionate zeal of Christian believers.

Gorky's brought the religious value of the passion of Christ into revolutionary thought and thus transcended and reaffirmed the hope for salvation. As I will demonstrate later, the process of redemption of the chief heroes--Pelageia Nilovna from a mute victim to a vocal revolutionary activist, and her son, Pavel, from a factory lad to a revolutionary leader--symbolizes the passion of Christ. What is poignant and powerful about Gorky's design is that he leaves no doubt about his agenda: the mother and son's rise from the silent, oppressed majority to the vocal, defiant minority, which has the clearly enunciated goal of bringing paradise on earth, fulfills every requirement for a Christian saint or martyr. No human frailty intrudes between them and their Christian ideal. It is in this notion of a person unblemished by any evildoing that Gorky has articulated his sense of the deed that propels the revolution to its heroic climax. These are the aspects of Gorky's *Mat'* I am going to consider.

The rhythm of martyrdom and inhuman perfection sets the tone of the narrative about Pavel, who comes to symbolize an apostle of the revolution.[4] The ritualistic trials of a young worker who, having been liberated from crippling fears and from the distrust and hatred of the people, is driven into revolutionary work carry the burden of awareness that the only promise of resurrection is in the act of heroic participation. Behind the solemn incantory rhythm of the May 1 demonstration, one hears the voice of Gorky preaching self-sacrifice and salvation.

> "Comrades," sang out Andrei, "we go on our own Golgotha for the sake of the new god, the god of light and truth, the god of reason and goodness! Our goal is far away, our crown of thorns is near! Those who do not believe in the power of truth, who do not have the courage to meet the death, who do not believe in themselves and are afraid of suffering--get aside!" (Gorky, in *Sobranie Sochinenii* 1960, 260)

The explicit references to Golgotha and the crown of thorns reveal Gorky as a tribune, an idealogist, and a prophet. The circular movement from the symbol of passion and sacrifice (Golgotha, the god of goodness) to Reason and Enlightenment (the god of reason and light) and back again to passion and sacrifice suggests an author torn between the powerful pull of the native image of the passion of Christ and Western rationalism and the Enlightenment. But the topography of the circular movement and the repeated emphasis on self-sacrifice also yield another important insight about Gorky's perceptions of deed.

Gorky was convinced in the transforming strength of the native image of the passion of Christ. Gorky found a means of persuasion in explaining the "resurrection" of Pelageia Nilovna as mother's love and Christian compassion. Curiously enough, his account of Pavel's "resurrection," presumably set into motion by social democrat agitation, is bleak, dreary and sounds hollow.

Gorky felt, as Tolstoy had felt, that a writer should be a preacher and a prophet of salvation. As a prophet, he forecasts the storm; as a preacher, he teaches moral values and castigates native shortcomings. The most dangerous shortcomings he detects are found in the native interpretation of the passion of Christ that emphasizes surrender and resignation. Gorky's own experience of poverty and want during his childhood and adolescence made him intimately acquainted with suffering and made him realize that the revolutionary spirit is animated neither by "the soul, complaining sadly, . . . nor by the soul, wandering and suffering, . . . rigid with fear" (ibid., 176). Gorky the preacher sees the inherent danger in the native celebration of freedom of will, which, in its eagerness and yearning for a heroic deed, indifferently "takes on both the good and the evil" (ibid.). The vibrations of Gorky's ideal spirit bear testimony to his acute sense of a deep-seated contradiction between

Russian cultural values and the values perpetuating the revolutionary thrust for redemption.

Like Tolstoy before him, Gorky moved toward moral insight of human endeavor. Although both of them celebrated the passion of Christ, it was Gorky who pinned his hopes of redemption not in the introverted parochialism of the past, but in the extroverted internationalism of the future. Gorky employed the combustive power of the literary plot to ignite popular anger and to serve as a moral guide to a new sociopolitical and cultural order. It is his sense of apostolic, rather than literary, mission which emerges from the pages of this novel. Gorky's evangelical fervor and belief in the Christian values of compassion and self-sacrifice defined his choice of the central figure. Gorky's chief protagonist is not the atheist Pavel, but his Christ-loving mother, whose obsessive self-effacing devotion to her son becomes the vehicle of her redemption.

The plot of *Mat'* is as uncomplicated as the process of Pelageia Nilovna's transformation into a revolutionary martyr. She is fearful, illiterate woman, who worriedly watches her son's growing alienation from other factory lads of his age. She finds out, to her utmost dismay and consternation, that her son has associated himself with the revolutionaries, the tsar murderers and avowed atheists. However, her fears are thwarted and her empathy towards the revolutionaries grows when she meets them in person.

The dialectic of ignorance and knowledge is dramatized by Gorky in order to sensitize the readers to their own impediments. Gorky's account of the mother's redemption is represented as inseparable from the process of enlightenment. The mother's encounter with the revolutionaries and her growing involvement in the dissemination of revolutionary literature among the factory workers parallel her growing awareness and understanding of the sources of evil in her past and present.

But, although Gorky's plea for enlightenment represents his support for active human participation in social change, the shift is effected by the irrational, by motherly love. Gorky might have forgone an account of Pavel's spiritual transformation because it mystified him as much as it did his readers, but he has painstakingly delineated Pelageia Nilovna's road to redemption. Moved by the desire to deflect suspicion from her arrested son, she takes over the distribution of revolutionary leaflets. Gorky sensed the revitalizing power of awakened human dignity that pulls itself up from fear to open defiance.

Pelageia Nilovna's process of redemption, however, echoes Gorky's own vacillation between his innate religious convictions and his acquired revolutionary beliefs.[5] The conflict reverberates through Pelageia Nilovna's painful grapple with her love for Jesus Christ and her disenchantment with the official Orthodox church. Her process of rebirth is accompanied by her reassessment of her religious belief. While her love for Jesus Christ remains untainted by doubt, the Church is cast off as corrupt and treacherous. The scene in which she visualizes her own redemption can be read as a symbolical severance of the umbilical cord between the religious believer and the church and marks the shift of Christian values into the realm of revolutionary activities.

> She walked past the mound along the road . . . and looked at her son. . . . She was ashamed to approach him, because she was pregnant. And in her arms she also had an infant. She went further. There were children, many of them, playing with a ball in the field, and the ball was red. The infant strained to reach the children and cried loudly. She gave him the breast and turned back; there on the mound stood soldiers, their bayonets pointed at her. She quickly ran to the church in the middle of the field, white, ethereal, as if built of the clouds, and terribly tall. A funeral service was on, the coffin was large, black, and tightly sealed. However, the priest and the deacon, in white vestments, walked around the church and sang: "Christ has risen from the dead!" Suddenly the priest screamed: "Take them!" His vestment vanished, his face had a grey severe moustache now. People scattered. . . . Mother dropped the infant on the floor. . . . She stood on her knees pleading with people to take her child. . . . She picked up the child and seated him on a cart (ibid., 272).

The visual image of Pelageia Nilovna is animated within a dense crowd of symbolic images of resurrection--pregnancy, baby, church, and the chant "Christ has risen!" It represents a violent push from a feeling of impotence into one of action and hope. Hope is far from radiant in Gorky, for he sounds a discordant final note in Mother's dream, where she suddenly falls into "the precipice which fearfully wails in her face"(ibid.). The fall, which follows the sense of hope, might be an indication of Gorky's persisting doubts about the possibility of redemption.

As happens occasionally throughout the novel, Gorky the writer, who reveals the darker sides of the human soul, overshadows Gorky the ideologist. His doubts resonate in the tension they create between the mother's skepticism about the frailties of human nature and her ardent belief in the value of martyrdom.

> In her heart of hearts, she did not believe that they [the revolutionaries] would be able to change life the way they wanted to and that they would be able to attract to their flame all the working people. Every-

one wants to have his belly full, but no one wants to put off until tomorrow what he can eat today. Only a few will follow this difficult
road, a few will see at its end the magic kingdom of fraternity of all
people (ibid., 229).

Although Pelageia Nilovna is suddenly struck with the thought that
"Christianity survived thanks to the martyrs who sacrificed their life for
Christ" (ibid., 261), I would suggest that it is Gorky himself who is
overwhelmed by this powerful argument. For Gorky, who looks at
revolutionary activities through the sympathetic eye of Pelageia Nilovna,
the revolutionaries' insistence on suffering and self-sacrifice is both
fascinating and scary. It is hardly a coincidence that Gorky's final acceptance of self-sacrifice, like Tolstoy's, is conveyed in almost exact biblical
reference: "You have to die to resurrect the people! Let thousands die,
so that thousands upon thousands can be resurrected! To die is easy.
Only if people could be could be resurrected! Only if people could rise!"
(ibid., 249).

Gorky's ambiguity resonates in the scene where Pavel gives his mother
the picture "The Resurrected Christ on the Way to Bethany" (ibid., 160).
And here we observe, as in the case of "Golgotha" and "the crown of
thorns" displayed prominently in the May 1 demonstration, symbolism
that is violated and effaced. The intentional eradication of the symbol
signals the break up of the literary plot and a conscious shift of the
narration into the political realm. Moreover, it makes explicit Gorky's
sense of identification between the religious messianism of Christ and
revolutionary work. Pelageia Nilovna, pondering over the irony of the
gift from a sworn atheist, feels "dissatisfied" and alienated from her son,
who "is not like other people, more like a monk." Here Gorky perceives
the revolutionaries as the transfiguration of Christ's apostles. Pelageia
Nilovna, he says, felt in the speeches of her son and his friends, "behind
the words denying God, a strong belief in him" (ibid., 191). Thus we
witness an embryonic shift in identification when the image of Christ is
being fleshed out of its representative vestige of power, namely the
church. Gorky's divided sympathies and ambiguity toward religion and
revolutionary deed merge the image of Christ with that of the revolutionary heroes and infuses revolutionary activities with religious
missionary fervor.

I take Gorky's reference to martyrdom as a major illustration of the
pain and uncertainty which enveloped his final, if unwilling, acceptance
of self-sacrifice. It emerges, under Gorky's inspection, as a crowning
effort of love and compassion for humankind.

The mother's heart warmed with the feeling of love for the unknown person, whom she conjectures as a strong man, full of inexhaustible power. He walks on the earth, cleansing with his labor-loving hands the eternal mould of lies, revealing to people a simple and clear truth of life. And this great truth, which *redeems* [emphasis added] all equity, welcomes everybody and promises freedom from greed, malice, and lying--the three monsters that have enslaved and scared the whole world with their cynical force (ibid., 356).

This vision is the frame for the process of redemption Gorky lays down before us. The process which began with a cowed, tongue-tied woman and culminates with a fearless, vocal tribune is complete. It echoes the intimate experience of the writer and revolutionary who rallied and agitated and was thrown into the dungeon of the notorious Petropavlovsk fortress.[6] In the final scene of the novel, Pelageia Nilovna has to take decisive steps on the way to her own Golgotha. She has to face the gendarmes as she carries a suitcase full of leaflets that contain the explosive antigovernment speech her son delivered in the courtroom. It is in the interplay of her old fears of beatings from the gendarmes and her desire to bring her son's word of truth to the people that Gorky's conception of the vital node for the break with the present is to be found. In this interplay, his convictions reveal themselves.

The cadence of her passionate plea for liberation from stiffening fear and indifference is sustained by an acrimonious denunciation of work. It manifests the author's genuine animosity toward work which sustains and perpetuates the system of its own oppression.

Poverty, hunger and disease--they are the fruit of our work. Everything is against us--we die every day, day after day, in work, in dirt, in lies; our labor feeds, fattens, and entertains others, while we are kept as dogs on a chain, illiterate--knowing nothing, in fear--afraid of everything! Our life is a night, a dark night!" (ibid., 403)

Gorky's hostility is sustained in the metaphors he employs to convey the image of human bondage and avarice: a factory is a "stone cage" with "greasy square eyes" (ibid., 153). The author's visual image of workers is as scathing as his portrayal of the factory. He intentionally lashes out at what he perceives to be the indignity of human complacency and surrender. The workers scurrying out of their houses are compared to "scared cockroaches," to "slag" (ibid.).

Gorky reinforces the already pervasive sense of antipathy toward industrial labor, which "sucks the workers dry of their energy and strength" and "brings them closer to death" (ibid.). He denies labor any positive merits and represents it as the culprit of workers' ills. Labor, Gorky insists, "deprives people of appetite and makes them resort to spirits, to stimulate the stomach with the burning sensations of vodka" (ibid., 154). Labor is the cause of "violence, savage child abuse, bloody fights, and occasional murders" (ibid.). But the force and degree of Gorky's censorship of labor should be measured against his celebration of labor as an integral part of Pavel's redemption.

Pavel's transformation from an ordinary factory lad into a revolutionary saint is accompanied by a conscientious attitude toward work. In sharp contrast to his derision of workers--"the slag," "the scared cockroaches"--Gorky's tone mellows and acquires laudatory notes when he speaks of Pavel, who "works hard, never skips work, and has never been fined" (ibid., 159).

The clash of contradictory statements could be somewhat alleviated if we distinguish here a polyphony of voices and interests. The voice of censorship belongs to a Russian and a Marxist ideologist, while the second voice belongs to a person who strains to represent the Western work ethic as the road to rebirth. Gorky the Russian saw labor as slavery and as a source of suffering. Gorky the Westerner leached out suffering and slavery from the imagery of labor. Gorky's rhetoric of work ethic, which is limp, colorless and sketchy against his vividly graphic and almost tangible scoff of labor, reveals his unease with the Western notion of work ethic. Labor, for Gorky, represents the process of redemption and perfection of the new man--Pavel, the revolutionary apostle.

In defining his credo of revolutionary work, Gorky claims that "people do not believe in words alone, we have to suffer, to wash our words in blood" (ibid., 198). He infuses the adopted Western theory of revolutionary reason with the Russian values of suffering and self-sacrifice.

It is in the interplay of the native image of the passion of Christ and the adopted Marxist theory of change, invigorated by the Lenin's theory of party organization,[7] that Gorky's relation to revolutionary work is to be found. Behind the scene of the revolutionaries' trial, in their defiance of the authority of the state and its legal system, lurks the image of Christ, who defied the authority of the high priests and their established custom of money changing in the outer court of the temple. Pavel's open declaration of his allegiance to the party is correlative, I believe, to Gorky's nascent conviction that the social democrats had become the voice of Christlike challenge to the injustices of the present.

But Gorky's novel does not culminate in the trial. For Gorky, as for his hero, Christ, the trial was a stepping-stone to a heroic self-sacrifice, a prelude to resurrection and the hope of salvation. The explosive rhythm in the closing scene of the novel depicts a thick crowd of people and the bloody, severely beaten Pelageia Nilovna, who passionately insists that "the soul that has been resurrected can't be murdered" (ibid., 404).

Having canvassed the spiritual transformation of his heroes, Gorky drew upon the currently popular Marxist view that consciousness is molded by human activity, *praxis*. Marx's celebration of human activity, however, was negotiated by the Russian drama of Salvation. A closer look at the name of one of Gorky's main protagonists, Pavel (Paul), the revolutionary spiritual leader of the workers, suggests an allusion to St. Paul, the spokesman of Christianity. Consequently, the author of the novel takes on the role of a literary spokesman for the new vision which has merged Western rationalism with Russian religious values. Gorky, the ideologist, imbibes the process of redemption and the birth of the new man with the Western notion of purposeful work, *praxis*, animated by the native conceptions of suffering and heroic self-sacrifice. The Western conception of human activity is invigorated by the Protestant notion of *calling* and *grace* and by the sense of hope of salvation embedded in the rigorous fulfillment of mundane activities. The Russian revolutionary conception of human activity, however, adapted the Western notion of *praxis* within the context of revolutionary activity alone. The Marxist notion of *praxis* breathed new life and meaning into the traditional Russian value of the heroic deed. Having endowed the heroic deed with the new motivational drive of revolutionary self-sacrifice, the Russian revolutionary viewed the whole scope of mundane activity as totally subjected and defined by the revolutionary goal of complete destruction.

It was the prerevolutionary Russian perceptions of work, which drew on the traditional image of the passion of Christ, that shaped the definition of work adopted from Western revolutionary thought. The innate kenotic[8] and eschatological visions of universal and absolute salvation, which were negotiated by the existing political institutions of autocracy, had effectively foreclosed any utilitarian and pragmatic notions of work. The meaning of labor was relegated to the act of sustaining life and to the metaphysical world of suffering.

Revolutionary theory filled in the moral vacuum left by the Russian Orthodox teaching which confined moral values to transcendental reality alone. The Russian revolutionary, who was concerned with transforming social reality, needed moral sanction and justification for his actions, which were directed at transforming his immediate social reality, the reality that was deemed irrelevant for salvation by the Russian Christian orthodoxy. The Russian revolutionary sought to anchor the Russian motivation to act and the sense of hope in his immediate social action. However, the thrust and motivation for salvation lay in the apocalyptic drive for destruction. The Russian perception of the passion of Christ, wedded to the Western secular theory of revolution, imparted a Russian meaning and energy to an otherwise alien enterprise and made the notion of revolutionary activity more accessible to Russians who were loath to forsake the image.

The Russian revolutionary intelligentsia, with Gorky as its spiritual leader, relegated the work ethic of the West to redemption and the hope for human perfection. Noble as it was, the motivation for work was kept suspended in future redemption and was divorced from immediate social reality. The Marxist revolutionary teaching of the value of work was planted in an intrinsically alien soil, devoid of the Western tradition of democracy and rationalism. In a paradoxical twist, the revolutionary activism of the Russian both saluted the redeemed man, the militant interventionist, the savior of the masses and immediately deprived him of independence under the iron rule of party discipline. The Russian revolutionary of the time celebrated the redemptive powers of work and denounced them as degrading. He insisted on rational thinking and immediately overturned it as detached and inhuman. The seeds of discord between an adopted ideology based on a rational conception of the value of work and the traditional emphasis in Russian thought on redemption and salvation were already imbedded in the early stages of the Russian revolutionary quest for change. The oscillation between Russian convictions and the adopted ideology of the West carried the Russian to the pinnacles of revolutionary heroic deeds and inhuman self-sacrifice and cast him into the abyss of tragic despair.

Part Two

Communist Work, The Glory,
and The Irony

6

The Bolsheviks' Visions of Communist Work

The question at issue is: shall we be able to work for ourselves? If we are not, I repeat, our republic must perish.

Vladimir Lenin [1]

The day after the Bolshevik coup in 1917, Vladimir Lenin, leader of the newly born Soviet republic, opened his address to the All-Russian Congress of Soviets with a promise to "construct the socialist order." [2] If the idea of socialist order was a rehash of Western liberal and Marxist theories, the visions energizing the process of "constructing the socialist order" were the product of Russian pressures. Unable to disengage themselves from the cultural webs of signification, the Bolsheviks harbored visions of work which strove to fuse the Russian value of heroic self-sacrifice with the Western value of productive efficiency.

Lenin's commitment to constructing a socialist society lent a distinctly Russian flavor to the Marxist idea of modernization. For all his devotion and loyalty to Marxism, Lenin refused to share his teacher's grudging admiration for the capitalist system of development. Unlike Marx, who looked upon a capitalist stage as a necessary prerequisite to a communist society, Lenin fervently believed that the evils of capitalist development could be bypassed, that underdeveloped, agrarian Russia could build socialism. Lenin's promise of socialism gave voice to the Russian traditional aversion to the Protestant value of the pursuit of gain. For the Russian set on achieving his eschatological dream of the heavenly kingdom the Western or Protestant emphasis on mundane economic activities, the deepest motivation for which was worry and care about the self, violated his sense of universal salvation and his conviction that mundane economic activities were worthless.

The Bolsheviks' adoption of the Marxist ideal of communist society reflected the point of convergence between the native Christian Orthodox and the Western liberal values of equality and justice. When Lenin in *The State and the Revolution* (1917) demanded to "free humanity from wage slavery" (Lenin in Z. L. Zile 1992, 87), he echoed Marx's call for "the destruction of the brazen law of wages by means of abolishing the system of wage-labor" (Behrends 1886, 48). The correlation of the notions of "wage" and "slavery" made prominent the underlying conviction about the evil and hostile nature of capitalist production and its institutions of property.

The call for destruction of the institution of property,--for nationalization of the largest enterprises[3] and consolidation of economic controls under the Supreme National Economic Council[4]--was accompanied by the leadership's growing concern with the workers' economic performance. The 1918 codification of work as "the duty of all citizens of the Republic,"[5] which was enshrined in the dramatic slogan "He who does not work, neither shall he eat!", represented a conscious attempt by the leadership to inculcate by the only means they knew--coercion and deprivation--in the Russian the new attitude to work.

Even though the Bolshevik maxim of "work as duty" bore a vague resemblance to the Western or Puritan work ethic, which "placed the dutiful pursuit of mundane activities in the center of the stage" (Giddens 1971, 127), this maxim sounded a sharp note of discord with the native value of work. The Russian penchant to view work either as suffering or as a heroic deed of self-sacrifice, which was influenced by Russia's prolonged history of tyrannical institutions, tended to make the Russian spurn mundane activity and to seek the promise of deliverance either in the past or in the future. The Western or Puritan work ethic, which had "productive efficiency" (ibid.) as its core value, was at odds with native Russian scorn for mundane activities.

In the tense drama of economic survival, the Bolshevik leaders of the Soviet republic, badly battered and torn by the civil war, found themselves increasingly preoccupied with the challenges of the Russian meaning of work. When Lenin emphatically threatened the death of the republic if people did not work for themselves, he gave voice to his deep-seated anxiety about the tradition of Russian hostility to productive work. This hostility continued in undiminished intensity and added apocalyptic tones to the growing number of warnings about the impending economic collapse of the Bolshevik state.

In reading the tomes of resolutions, speeches, and directives about the shifts in economic policies from War Communism (1918-1920)[6] to New Economic Policy (1921-1928), and later to Stalin's First Five-Year Plan of industrialization and collectivization (1928-1933), it is informative to observe the tone and the underlying perceptions of work emanating from those documents. If Lenin's rhetoric during War Communism extolled the virtues of heroic, selfless work in the name of the Soviet republic, his later advocacy of partial restoration of free trade, private entrepreneurship, and commerce revealed a grudging admission that not universal aspirations, but one's "own interest," "a jolt and motivation" driven by "a market," provides "a stimulus"[7] for productive work. The exigency of economic survival forced the leaders of the Soviet state, Lenin and Stalin, to pay heed, if qualified by their own cultural perceptions, to the Western, Protestant value of efficiency.

The implied dissonance between the native perceptions of work and the Bolshevik leaders' visions of communist work lay at the heart of the ensuing, protracted process of negotiations between the Russian and his new leaders. It was a negotiation about wedding the native image of self-sacrifice and the heroic deed to the Western ethic of work. In this negotiation, the chief voices in creating a new communist ethic of work belonged to Lenin, Bukharin, and Stalin.

Logically, I must begin with Vladimir Lenin (1870-1924), the author and the leader of the Russian revolutionary redemption and the founder of Russian Bolshevism. There is an ironic twist in Russian cultural history in the fact that Lenin, who was raised to the status of secular saint in Soviet Russia, was named after Vladimir, the saint *who was the first Christian ruler of Russia*.

Vladimir Lenin, born Ul'ianov, who represented the very embodiment of missionary zeal for communist redemption, understood the function of work as an unquestioning devotion to duty, diligence, and application. This understanding reflected the temperament and convictions of his Orthodox father, Il'ia Nikolaevich. An article in *Vestnik Evropy* (1876), a metropolitan St. Petersburg paper, spoke about Lenin's father, who was an inspector of education in Simbirsk Province, as a "rare, exceptional phenomenon" and, in describing his tireless efforts in the face of difficulty and apathy, said, "Such strength and vigor can come only from a devotion bordering on abnegation" (Wolfe 1964, 47). The language of the article resonates with the temper and tone of the passion of Christ, as does the image of the man it portrays. Il'ia Nikolaevich's work ethic seemed almost an exact replica of the work ethic of the Christian ascetics that was propounded by Sergei Bulgakov in 1909. An official epitaph of him written by N. Delarov, the deputy from Simbirsk to the second Duma (March-June 1907), is in the voice of Russian Orthodox social heritage, the heritage which received its ultimate expression in Lenin's perceptions of the communist ethic of work. Delarov extolled I. N. Ul'ianov as a man whose "personal aim in life . . . [was] zeal in serving the good of the people" (ibid., 50). It was Lenin's older sister Anna who detected a striking similarity between her father's and Vladimir's "love of work and . . . quick temper" (ibid., 43). Lenin's tactical adroitness and vituperative oratory were coupled with intense single-mindedness, industriousness, and practicality and were energized by a missionary zeal for communist redemption. He turned to revolutionary activities after his elder brother was executed for attempting to assassinate the tsar in 1887.

A diligent student of Marxism, Lenin traveled to Western Europe in 1895 to familiarize himself with other disciples. In Germany he met Karl Kautsky, editor of *Die Neue Zeit*, and the aging Friedrich Engels. Among his most cherished purchases was the third volume of Marx's *Capital*, which had just been issued by Engels from Marx's posthumous notes. In partaking of the wisdom Marx's *Capital,* Lenin might have marveled with Marx at the ascetic ethic of Protestantism, which "chang[ed] almost all the traditional holidays into workdays" (Loomis and Rytina 1970, 92). It is impossible to know whether he enjoined in Marx's measured compassion for the capitalist martyrs, whom Marx wished for "the simple dictates of humanity . . . released from this martyrdom and temptation in the same way that the Georgian slave owner was lately delivered, by the abolition of slavery" (ibid.). If Lenin could identify with any aspect of the Protestant martyrs, it would be the intensity of their ascetic devotion, which was nurtured by suffering and self-sacrifice, core values in the Russian perception of human activity.

Upon his return to Russia, Lenin became the moving force in unifying all of the splintered Marxist groups. After his arrest and exile to Siberia, Lenin left Russia for Western Europe to spread revolutionary ideas and fan the flames of popular discontent. At the height of the World War I, heartened by the collapse of the Russian monarchy, Lenin returned to Russia to lead the Bolshevik party to political power.

Having become leader of the socialist republic, Lenin passionately believed, as Marx had before him, that under new economic conditions-- when the proletariat became the chief executive of political and economic control, when economic greed was no longer be a driving force--a brand new attitude to word work would come into existence. He gave voice to a new vision of work ethic--communist labor. Molded by his vision and animated by his passion, communist labor became for Lenin the ultimate tool in achieving salvation, the consummation of a universal dream.

Lenin's vision of communist society was an exact replica of the Western Marxist ideal of a classless society, in which the "the brazen law of wages" is "abolished" and "spoliation in any form" is "removed" (Behrends 1886, 47), but this vision was animated by the Russian value he cherished and knew, heroic self-sacrifice.

Amidst the economic collapse of the war-ravaged republic, threatened by the White armies led by Alexander Kolchak and Anton Denikin, Lenin felt that the hope for socialist order lay in selfless volunteer work for the benefit of society. He hailed the valiant decision of the Communists at the Moscow-Kazan Railroad, "not to stint their health and life for the gains of the revolution" and "to help to achieve victory over Kolchak"[8] by working six hours without pay on Saturdays. Lenin was convinced that this kind of enthusiasm and determination represented the "shoots" (*GB*, 437) of the new work ethic and demonstrated the new socialist order in the making. Economic chaos was redeemed by self-sacrifice and the heroic deed, labeled the "Communist sabbath." And this was the lesson Lenin wanted the others to learn. It was his own secularized version of faith, wrapped in Marxist vestiges of class conscience. Self-sacrifice and heroism were the faith, and conscience provided the reason.

Lenin was an irascible proponent of altruistic work and said that he felt that social work would be smothered if it were animated by material benefits, by "rewards" and "fixed rates." In his speech on April 8, 1920,[9] "Communist labor," he said,

is labor performed gratis for the benefit of society, labor not performed as a definite duty, not for the purpose of obtaining a right to certain products, not according to previously established and legally fixed rates but voluntary labor, irrespective of rates, labor performed without expectation of reward, without the condition of reward, labor performed out of habit of working for the common good, and out of a conscious realization [which becomes a habit] of the necessity of working for the common good--labor as the requirement of a healthy body (Lenin 1937, 447).

The matchless cadence of Lenin's biting criticism of his political opponents, who accused him of "utopianism," underscored, I believe, his preference for the drama of belief rather than for cool detached rationality. In drawing up his definition of unalienated, communist labor, Lenin reaffirmed Tolstoy's postulate that human labor springs from psychological and physiological rather than economic needs. Both great Russians celebrated labor--the heroic deed of self-sacrifice--as the ultimate expression of belief in Christlike human perfection, untarnished by human desires and by human weaknesses, driven utterly by the sense of social responsibility.

In articulating his vision of the communist work ethic, Lenin employed the image he knew best, that of his father and other representatives of the Russian intelligentsia who, "devotedly filled up unremunerated posts to built up Russian science and culture" (Wolfe 1964, 44). But there also loomed behind this belief the Russian yearning for the transcendental ideal, the miraculous, which (in the spirit of the passion of Christ) would lead to and bring salvation.

The drama of the fight for salvation inexorably tied the process of endowing labor with the heroic features of self-sacrifice. The revolutionary martyrs, Lenin intoned, "bring about a change in the mood of the masses, by the heroic initiative of individual groups which, on the background of such change in the mood of the masses, often play a decisive role" (*GB*, 438).

For Lenin, as for Tolstoy, the call for altruistic, self-sacrificial, heroic labor represented a Russian challenge to the profit-oriented Western work ethic. But Lenin went a step further. Unlike Tolstoy, whose ideas remained untested, Lenin faced the social reality of a gap between the ideological heights of the communist work ethic and the daily activities of the workers. Although he bitterly admitted that "our society, our social system, are still a very long way from the broad, genuinely mass application of this form of labor" (*FD*, 44), his was the bitterness of a prophet speaking in the desert. But it also exhibited that determination of the Russian folk hero who sought salvation by whatever means.

Lenin visualized socialization of the Russian worker in the communist labor ethic through volunteer and cohesive labor: "Subbotniks, labor armies, labor service . . . the various forms of Socialist and Communist labor" (ibid.). The tone of his prescriptions was as emphatic and revealing as its content. Lenin's belligerent invocation of coercion, which was later perfected in Stalin's labor camps, as means of socialization in the communist ethic of labor--as exemplified by the terms "labor army" and "labor service"--articulated socialist Russia's road to salvation and the demand for sacrifice.

In the fall of 1921, surveying the economic collapse and faced with the mounting problems of hunger and peasant unrest, Lenin refused to surrender to the growing sense of despondency. With determination to overcome the despair and the tensions lying behind it, he enlarged on the value of suffering to ease his countrymen's pain and disappointment at the collapse of War Communism. He tried to reassure the Russians that the promise of communism was still alive, although removed into a more distant future.[10]

> If the Communists put the question of the New Economic Policy intel-
> ligently, there cannot be the slightest doubt in their minds that we suf-
> fered a very severe defeat on the economic front. And it is inevitable,
> of course, that some people should become despondent . . .
>   Did not the Red Army retreat? It started its victory by fleeing from
> the enemy. . . it turned out that after we had been thoroughly thrashed
> once, and sometimes more than once, we justified the proverb: *"One
> who has been thrashed is worth two who have not"* [emphasis added].
> After being thrashed, we began to advance slowly, systematically and
> and cautiously. (*NEP*, 259)

Lenin's transcendent optimism sprang from his personal experience
as the leader of an insignificant revolutionary group which he brought
almost single-handedly to the pinnacle of political power. Moreover, the
traditional Russian belief in the benefits of pain and suffering, which is
exemplified by the proverb "A man who has been thrashed is worth two
who have not," invigorated and sustained Lenin's innate optimism and
combative spirit through the rigors of post-war reconstruction and the
physical pain of the bullet that remained lodged in his neck since August
1918.

It was perhaps his acute awareness of the breadth of despair seizing
the people that gave power and vigor to Lenin's plea. The metaphor of
"the economic front" draws on an implicit link between political and
economic survival. The metaphor communicates the essence of labor,
the pattern of which was coterminous with army rule and discipline: "We
say, as we said in the army: Those who want to cause our destruction
must perish, and here we shall adopt the sternest disciplinary measures;
and we shall save our country, and our republic will live" (*NEP*, 267).

It was this explicit collusion of ideological cajolery and stern threats,
which flowed from the implicit mortal danger to the Bolshevik state, that
gave rhythm and shape to the Soviet history of rebuilding and reconstruction. The whole flurry of telegrams, written instructions, vehement accusations, and excoriations were directed at the urgency of the immediate
situation. It was a daily paradox, which caused Lenin irrepressible ire
and anguish, that his painstaking, superhuman effort to bring practicality
and hard work into his government had hardly any effect.[11]

Unlike the passion of the Russian intellectuals that was fanned by
moral concerns and theoretical abstractions, Lenin's passion was continu-
ously invigorated by the heroic deed and the practical process of redemption. Herein may lie the key to his success as an organizer and a leader,

as well as the source of his continuous struggle for practicality. His almost panic-stricken letter to Sokol'nikov, a member of the collegium of the commissariat for finance, of January 22, 1922, gives voice to his ongoing quarrel with the members of his government.

> What I mortally fear is that you, now *actually in charge* of the *most important* People's Commissariat, will be carried away with restructuring, reorganization, and the theoretical line (you do have a weakness on this score)--instead of practice, practice and practice: raising trade, *increasing and collecting taxes,* restoring the ruble. Really and truly I am in mortal fear of this; do not succumb to this weakness, otherwise we shall collapse. (Lenin 1970, 446)

Yet Lenin's very difficulty in coping with his comrades' flight into theories made the quarrel agonizingly contemporary. Lenin made a superhuman attempt to rid his surroundings of the evils of the culture, of the intellectual's escape from the pains of immediate social reality and the peasant's unabated attempts to manipulate the hostile environment.

Lenin's sublimated celebration of altruistic labor of 1920 acquired more somber, darker tones in 1921 and 1923. A powerful figure of intense passions and the very embodiment of self-sacrifice, Lenin understood the function of work ethic as the means of economic and political survival. Although Lenin, following Marx, believed that change in social reality would bring change in the worker's conscience and his attitude to work, Russian reality proved otherwise. The grim facts of the day-- workers' strikes, their desertion of workplace, and the fall in production --bore bitter testimony to the illusory nature of Lenin's vision of the communist ethic of work. Lenin's call for a change in attitude, "You worked for the capitalist, for the exploiter, and of course, you worked badly, but now you are working for yourself, for the workers' and peasants' government" (*NEP,* 267), exposed the tragic irony of betrayed expectations. Lenin's plea resounded with the consternation and surprise of an ideologue whose assumptions were rebuffed by the workers, whom, he believed, stood to benefit the most.

Forced to overcome his inner hostility to the capitalist West, in 1921 Lenin, who was a wily politician, was determined to learn from the enemy. If the Lenin of 1894 was "infuriated" by Petr Struve's[12] conclusion that the Russians had "to confess" their "lack of culture, and turn to capitalism for instruction," the Lenin of 1921 repeated this conclusion word for word. (Wolfe 1964, 122) Driven by practical considerations in what might have been a valiant attempt to overcome his and his countrymen's distaste for the capitalist West, Lenin extended himself to exploit each indication of the strength of the West as the source of salvation for Soviet Russia. Speaking to the All-Russian Congress of Political Education Departments on October 17, 1921, Lenin boldly conceded Russia's cultural and social inadequacy for meeting the demands of communist society. Although critical of the West, he recognized the Western value of work.

> The capitalists . . . and the foreign capitalists, concessionaires and leaseholders . . . will knock hundreds per cent of profit out of you, they will enrich themselves by your side. Let them. Meanwhile you will learn from them the art of management, and only when you do that will you be able to build up a Communist republic. (*NEP*, 267)

If the vision of "a Communist republic" had become the stuff of the future, in the immediate present the Russian ethic of work, according to Lenin, had to "combine . . . revolutionary enthusiasm . . . with the ability to be an efficient and literary merchant."[13] Lenin's bent on fusing Russian passion with Western rationality extended to his embracing the Western art of management, "the adoption of much that is scientific and progressive in the [efficient management] system of [Frederick W.] Taylor, and the coordination of earnings with the overall performance of factories."[14] The author and indispensable mover of the Bolshevik revolution, tormented by disease and approaching death, desperately tried to invigorate his fading illusion with the Western value of efficiency.

If we study the events of Lenin's posthumous deification not in the isolation of personal perceptions, but in the context of a painful transition from a preindustrial to a modernizing society, it is difficult to shake off the impression that the figure of Lenin filled in the psychological vacuum left by the disintegration of Christian orthodox belief. It was none other than Stalin, a non-Russian and a nonintellectual, who understood better than any Russian intellectual the tag and pull of the Russian native image of the heroic martyr. But first I will turn my attention to Nikolai Bukharin.

Although the age of promise was the age of glorious visions of a perfect society, those visions receded imperceptibly into a more distant future. The promise of a perfect society, a "heavenly kingdom on earth," yielded surreptitiously to a less glamorous vision of a "transitional, socialist, period." In conceptualizing his vision of communist work, Nikolai Bukharin (1888-1938), a leading party spokesman and the editor-in-chief of the Bolshevik newspaper *Pravda* from 1917 to 1929, blended the Russian drama of passion with the Marxist theory of class struggle, and with Lenin's theory of proletarian dictatorship and class conscience.

Bukharin looked with vigor upon a class-oriented morality, "a starting point in our work, which determines the rules of human behavior." (*S*, 45) Bukharin's identifying position, which represented the core and, indeed, the whole of the socialist ideology of work, was the absolute opposition of the proletarian state and its antagonists, whom he lumped together as "the class-opponents." He was not willing merely to sound the acrimonious call to "nurture an absolutely instinctive reaction of passionate hatred toward our class-opponents"; Bukharin wanted "the passion of hatred" to consummate the work for "the socialist ideal." (ibid.)

Bukharin's conception of socialization represented a curious process of energizing the public toward work and was highly Russian in its animating human activity by passion. The age of promise was, indeed, fraught with glaring inconsistencies and ironies, for looming over the virulent invectives against class-opponents was Bukharin's extraordinarily telling argument that "a conscientious attitude toward work" (*S*, 46) should be learned from the very "class-opponents." His argument echoed Lenin's call to learn from the class enemy.

This paradox--the emergent absorption with the work ethic, and the expressed desire to learn from the class that had been declared doomed to defeat[15]--was propelled by Bukharin's growing despair over the gap between his vision of communist work and the Russian's attitude to word work. More than anyone else, Bukharin typified the irony of the vision, which was animated by a class-oriented mentality. The poetic visionary of the work ethic, animated by class strife fell, a victim of his own advocacy of hatred, animated by class struggle.[16]

Although both Lenin and Bukharin, in a wondrous leap of faith, envisioned the glory of an unalienated, class-oriented ethic of work, Stalin bore no illusions. The wily tactician of Russian industrial redemption deftly manipulated the Russian image of the Passion of Christ to achieve his own ends. In a speech given in April 1924, Stalin stated,

What I have in mind is style in the work, . . . which give[s] rise to the special type of the Leninist worker. Leninism is a school of theory and practice which trains a special type of worker for the Party and the state and creates a special Leninist style in work . . .

There are two special features: a. the wide Russian revolutionary range of action and b. American efficiency. The Leninist style combines these two special features in Party and state work (*F*, 101-2).

Tapping into the prevailing mood of loss and the need for a sacred image, Stalin set out to infuse the popular spirit with the urgency of the day and to make Lenin and his style of work the symbol of a new work ethic. Although Lenin believed in the Christlike perfectibility of human nature, Stalin suffered no such illusions. A rebellious outcast of the Tiflis Theological Seminary, Stalin nonetheless grudgingly admired the Jesuits for being "systematic and persevering in working to achieve their sordid ends" (Rigby 1966, 38).

It might well be that his admiration for Jesuit efficiency lay at the core of Stalin's idea of communist work. Stalin took as his subject what he perceived as the ultimate expression of the "systematic and persevering in working"--efficiency. Stalin's celebration of efficiency, which enlarged on Lenin's frequent despair over what the latter perceived as the Bolshevik's leaders impracticality and preoccupation with theories,[17] was also intended, I believe, to undermine his political opponents. It was Stalin, "the man of action, rather than a creative thinker" (ibid., 23), who identified with American pragmatism and emphasized the American brand of efficiency as the premium core value of a Soviet ideology of work. But Stalin's sense of pragmatism was highly eclectic. In Stalin's interpretation, American efficiency was reduced to "an indomitable spirit," a spirit which "neither knows nor will be deterred by any obstacle, that plugs away with businesslike perseverance until every impediment has been tackled even if it be of minor importance" (F, 103). Stalin's vision of communist work, filtered through the prism of the native image and fleshed out with its core values, may be seen as a refraction of the familiar theme of the passion of Christ.

In his desire to cut through to a primary definition of efficiency, Stalin leaned heavily on the negative. It might also be that the leader of the Soviet state could not find in the Russian vocabulary the appropriate words to explain the meaning of efficiency. Stalin was not given to much talk, and if he abruptly reverted from the celebration of American efficiency to a dire warning against the crippling effect of its "narrow practicality and unprincipled commercialism" (F, 103), he made explicit the boundaries of the amalgamated vision of communist work, which severely punished any private ventures. The wedding of Russian revolutionary spirit and American efficiency attested to Stalin's growing realization that, his loathing of it notwithstanding, he could no longer ignore capitalism's achievements.

It is an ultimate historic irony that the American work ethic, the epitome of capitalist entrepreneurship, was adopted by the Russian revolutionary leader as the crux of a new communist work ethic. Stalin's adroit movement between the mutually exclusive notions of the self-effacing revolutionary deed and self-assertive American efficiency gave pitch and tone to the process of negotiation between the native and adoptive values of work. Stalin ostensibly sought to instill the value of American efficiency, which he saw as an "antidote" against the evils of traditional Russian "inertness . . . and revolutionary phrase-mongering" (*F*, 102). The air was filled with drama, the drama of heightened passions of fear, insecurity, and idealistic fervor, which was craftily orchestrated Stalin to speed industrialization.

In a speech to industrial managers in 1931, Stalin fixed attention on speed, *the tempo* of production, and invoked the specter of political and cultural disaster if work was not animated by "the passionate Bolshevik desire to master the science of production" (*SP*, 124). His speech was emotionally electrifying in its emphasis on universal salvation. "It is impossible to reduce the tempo!" intoned Stalin. "It is necessary as far as possible to accelerate it. . . . This is dictated to us by our obligations to the working class of the whole world" (ibid.).

To conclude, the Bolshevik leadership's attempts to celebrate the mutually exclusive notions of self-effacing revolutionary deed and self-assertive American efficiency, of self-sacrifice and mercantile rationality, of altruism and work-incentives, reveal with an unusual power and clarity the Bolshevik leadership's ambivalence toward Western values of work. What makes their ambivalence particularly poignant is that, despite their disturbing awareness of the debilitating effects of the Russian image, they themselves remained deeply entangled in the cultural webs of signification created by this image.

Yet there remained questions about the Russians' perceptions of the postrevolutionary drama and about how they negotiated their leaders' call for a new work ethic. There was still the question of how the visions of the Bolshevik leaders would inspire believers in the age of promise, how the story of the passion of Christ would evolve in the industrializing society.

7

The New Christians in the Soviet Industrialization: Gladkov, Kataev, Makarenko

In sketching the emergent drama urged on Soviet writers by the Leninist-Stalinist industrialization policies, I have focused on Russians who believed in the age of revolution. According to the believers, "heroism, self-sacrifice and universal salvation" were the primary values of a new, communist man. When this conviction became articulate in Fedor Gladkov's *Cement* (1921-1924), Valentin Kataev's *Time, Forward!* (1932), and Anton Makarenko's *The Pedagogical Poem* (1925-1935), the Russian notion of communist work once and for all took on all the attributes of the passion of Christ and became a Soviet myth.

A heroic personality overcoming the enormous hurdles of traditional inertia, apathy, and bureaucratic authority was seen as the true representative character of the ensuing drama of the evolution of New Man. As for materials and resources, the Russian was exhorted to perform heroic deeds and draw on the visions of the Bolshevik leadership. The visions, interpreted as a marshalling of resources for the survival and ultimate universal victory of Bolshevik ideals, were primarily aimed at a broad social transition to modernity and were economic, social, and cultural. The issue of transition was not sharply drawn until 1928, when it became a stern demand for an organized effort in all areas of social life to ensure speedy industrialization.

From 1921 to 1924, at the time of the New Economic Policy (NEP), it seemed to Fedor Gladkov (1883-1958) that the matter of the Bolshevik revolution--social equality in a brand new society created by New Men, animated by the communist spirit of work--was precariously close to collapse. Gladkov, a writer and professional teacher who had been an active Bolshevik since 1904,[1] a Red Army volunteer during Wrangel's assault in 1920, and a tireless organizer of schools for illiterate workers in Novorosiisk,[2] felt perturbed by the economic policy of allowing a significant private economy and foreign concessions. To his dismay, he watched helplessly as the revolutionary fervor of War Communism, however harsh and brutal it had been, yielded to petty squabbles and a fight for power within the Party. Nonetheless, Gladkov was not convinced that the revolutionary dream was dead. Lenin's call for active participation in socialist construction lifted his sagging belief and filled him with a determination to write and educate. Undaunted by his expulsion from the party in 1921 on charges of behaving like "a typical intelligentsia" (Ul'rikh 1982, 47), Gladkov, with Gorky's support, moved to Moscow to start his literary career and manage an evening school for workers. Gladkov, who had been member of *Kuznitsa*, the Moscow group of proletarian writers, since 1921, felt that if the evils of the NEP were to be overcome, if the communist salvation was to come, both could be achieved only by the New Man, the purveyor of the new ethic of labor. Gladkov's *Cement* ushered in a host of literary visions of the New Man and the communist labor of Kataev and Makarenko.

Like Gladkov, Valentin Kataev (1897-1986) moved to Moscow in the early 1920s to become a professional writer. He earned his daily bread by writing for a worker's newspaper entitled *Gudok (The Whistle)*. Kataev, however, did not experience the powerful pull of Bolshevik ideology, as Gladkov did. Writing in 1928 about his activities during the civil war, he admitted to being "toss[ed] from the Whites to the Reds, from the counterrevolution to the Cheka."[3] Throughout the 1920s, Kataev felt at ease to pursue his own literary visions and to stay away from any political affiliations. Like other "fellow-travelers," Kataev was a writer who "gave tacit assent to the Soviet regime but who stopped short of actively supporting it" (Russel 1981, 18). However, with the abolition of NEP and the beginning of a frenzied campaign of Stalinist industrialization "from above,"[4] writers were exhorted to "throw themselves into the thick of the building program, go to the village and to the construction site, . . . gain material for creative work with and amongst the proletarians and so re-educate themselves."[5] One can only speculate whether visits to construction sites were made in a sincere desire to get involved or in fear of repercussions. That is of no concern of mine. I am interested in Kataev's perceptions of people and their work, which he witnessed at the Rostov Agricultural Machinery Plant and the Stalingrad Tractor Factory (ibid., 22). Having spent a year (from May 1931 to the spring of 1932) at Magnitogorsk, in the Urals, Kataev marveled with pride and exhilaration at human might and its ability to change the social and the natural environment. He wrote, "To see with one's own eyes how our country is being transformed from an agrarian land into an industrial one results in a change in one's outlook as a writer" (ibid.). Kataev's enthusiasm spilled over in *Time, Forward*, an ode to the New Man and his communist labor.

Gladkov and Kataev's celebration of the New Man and his labor represented an artistic celebration of a vicarious experience; however, the professional educator and writer, Makarenko (1889-1939) in *The Pedagogical Poem,* gave voice to the pangs and joys of his own experience in creating what he perceived to be the New Man from a criminal and a delinquent.

If Gladkov, Kataev, and Makarenko responded with vigor to the Party's call for "creative work with and among the proletarians," their exuberant celebration of the New Man and his labor was more often than not overshadowed by doubt. However muted by ardent optimism, the doubt still exploded in the emotional collusion between the real and the illusory, between the Russian image of work as the refraction of the passion of Christ and the Bolshevik leadership's visions of Western-like efficiency and rationality.

Gladkov was among the first Soviet writers of significance to enunciate a Soviet version of the passion of Christ with its hypnotic and potentially fatal fascination with the Bolshevik vision. In Gladkov's narrative, *Cement*, which bristles with emotion and poetic impressionism, a New Communist Woman, Dasha, casts off her past life, in which she was a loving wife and a devoted mother, and transforms herself into a woman with a heightened sense of social responsibility, and Dasha's husband, Gleb, a New Communist Man, single-handedly organizes workers to restore a forsaken cement plant. Gleb and Dasha, two dramatic self-reliant figures untarnished by human weaknesses and indecision, introduce a host of literary visions of the Christlike figures of Kataev and Makarenko. These New Men valiantly stand their ground against enormous odds and finally declare victory, but not unless they have paid a heavy price in self-sacrifice.

Curiously, the New Man and the New Woman are a refraction of the prerevolutionary image of rebirth. They are young rebels who broke with the past and its burdens of personal and intimate attachments. I call such figures the *New Christians* in two senses. First, the heroes, like the proverbial converts to Christianity, seem to challenge existing social behavior. Second, they are animated by social goals which demand that they, like Christian converts, should transcend the mundane human needs of love and social attachments. Those figures, which stand above the crowd and are ferociously independent, are driven by social ideals and undefiled by personal ambition. They represent the martyred image of the Russian retouched by Western self-reliance.

In this chapter, I look closely at three Soviet novels. I find it useful to begin with Gladkov's *Cement*. This novel, according to Marc Slonim,[6] an incisive observer of the Russian literary scene, enjoyed "a tremendous success" in the mid-1920s because a Russian reader "demands social and moral inspiration."[7] In Gladkov's novel the heroes, the creators of communist work, make their appearance while they are still entangled in the ethos of violence, inhuman suffering, martyrdom, and heroic altruism of War Communism.

> G. "We are a people of ruthless deeds, and our thoughts and feelings are conditioned by necessity and indisputable historical truth."
> K. "Here is a terrible beast and a great creation . . . all in one. . . . Why? . . . Among you there are so many martyrs, but there are also so many villains and monsters."
> G. "Let it be so. But we go into eternity. The villains will be forgotten, but we will be remembered as creators and heroes. Immortality is death and blood" (Gladkov 1931, 276-77).

Cement describes the triple process of becoming a New Christian. On one level is the process of moral purification, as expressed by analogy in the tempestuous breakdown of the husband and wife relationship between Gleb and Dasha. On the social level, it is the process whereby Gleb and Dasha surrender their private life to a public life. On the personal level, it is the process of self-imposed solitude and self-effacement. The vibrations of that process bear testimony to Gladkov's intimate knowledge of the tensions besetting the process of rebirth. He leads his heroes in their transfiguring experience into an environment dense with the gory specters of evil--torture, rape, thievery, and betrayal. It is the environment of a creeping, stultifying bureaucracy, of a fight for power within the Party, of commercialism, and of budding industrial reconstruction--the Russia of the New Economic Policy (1921-1928). It is the environment where the new ethic of work resonates with Lenin's and Bukharin's passionate pleas for self-sacrifice, for overcoming the evils of bureaucracy, class conscience, and class struggle.

The opening scene of *Cement* is the paradigm of the dramatic image in postrevolutionary Russian literature. In that scene, all that seemed hostile and treacherous in Russian reality became exposed. The opening overture, which is exuberant and tense with coiled emotions, betrays dark overtones. The story opens with the scene of return. Gleb Chumalov, a Red Army commissar and a former cement plant worker, comes home after three years of civil war only to discover that his past has been erased and his present is trampled. The plant lies in ruins. It is through Gleb's eyes that the reader takes in the deceptively familiar and tranquil sight of the plant and the workers' huts, where "three years seem as though it were only yesterday: nothing has changed" (ibid., 7). But the placid veneer is ripped by the shocking sight of "the gracious outlines of the electricity transmission towers, chimneys, taller than the mountains, the multitude [of] wire strings," defiled by wandering goats, pigs, and roosters, which spread "like a mold" (ibid., 9). The sense of alienation intensifies when Gleb encounters some women from the factory. The older one "looks like a *baba-iaga* (hag), and two younger ones are *bosiatskogo vida* (looking like tramps) (ibid., 9).

The conflict expands and explodes in a volley of crushed expectations when Gleb faces his wife, Dasha, only to find out that she is a stranger he has never known before. The woman whom he has been yearning to see after three years of separation "breaks loose, stands on her feet, and casts at him a distrustful, cunning glance" (ibid., 12). The next moment she leaves him for a two-day business trip, but not before telling him that their young daughter is in an orphanage. She, Dasha, had to place her there to be able to attend to her work. Dasha explains that she herself eats in a public canteen and comes home only to spend the night.

A sense of catastrophe and irretrievable loss besieges Gleb. His vision of an "empty nest" is intertwined with the specter of "a lackluster forsaken plant." The action of the novel springs from the underlying suggestion that return is a mirage, that the life Gleb has returned to has changed beyond repair. Gleb wanders about the ghost of the plant, shattered by the scope of devastation and the feeling of betrayal of his memories of a mighty plant and of himself, a proud worker. In this scene, as throughout the novel, Gladkov manipulated the only literary conventions he knew, the conventions of the Marxist ideology of man's alienation in industrialized society, of Lenin's ideology of class struggle, and of Russian romanticism.

Gladkov exploited these conventions in a narrative in which he managed to convey his personal sense of man's response to social reality. Since his personal sense reveals continuity with many other perceptions of man's work--for example, those of Gorky and Andreev--we may accept it as distinctly Russian in outline. Like Gorky and Andreev before him, Gladkov felt that to work meant to "conquer" the world by the power of the spirit. The ritualistic redemption of young believers into the brand new world--the matter of the passion of Christ--was equivalent to the travails of the revolutionary martyrs of Andreev and Gorky.

Gladkov's image of work, however, was in the ongoing process of negotiation between Russian traditional values of suffering and self-sacrifice and the Bolsheviks' vision of efficient and rational work. Gladkov's wrenching doubts come to a head in the clash between the Western rationality of Kleist, the russified German engineer, who ran the plant before the revolution, and Gleb, a worker and the moving spirit behind the reconstruction of the plant. The conversation between Kleist and Gleb will be recalled. Gleb, brimming with pride, points out to Kleist that they repaired the machine in three days, as he Gleb had prophesied, and not in a month, as Kleist had suggested.

K. "Yes, yes. With this scope of work you've performed miracles. But this is an enormous waste of work force: there is no planning, no organized divison of labor. Enthusiasm is like a downpour: it is short-lived, harmful."

G. "It is a very important factor, comrade technical manager. With enthusiasm we move mountains. When everything is destroyed, enthusiasm is vital. As soon as we revive all this stuff, then we will learn, according to plan, the production process" (ibid., 168).

If Gladkov was responsive to the attractions of the Western values of work and to the need for rationality, he also understood the grounds for the Russian preoccupation with romantic enthusiasm. Gladkov endowed a German, not a Russian, with Western rationality. This might have been because he was acutely aware of the Russian aversion to rationality and pragmatism, an aversion which was rooted in Russian Orthodoxy. Gladkov retained this distrust of rationality as a part of the symbol of work. Gladkov felt that with the emphasis on rationality, bureaucratization grew rampant and the dark shadows of the tsarist bureaucracy of the past became the haunting reality of the present. It is in Gleb's continuous clashes with bureaucratic organizations that the treacherous and hostile nature of rationality discloses itself: "damned bureaucracy, to make it work, you have first to break it" (ibid., 114).

But Gladkov's quarrel with bureaucracy could not foreshadow his growing doubts about the value of passion in a world where the Russian, a perennial outsider and rebel, became an insider and a participant in the process of industrialization. It is a sign of Gladkov's divided perceptions that a politician and career party man, Zhidkii, concludes that, "The romance of fierce battle has died. Today we need cold, calculating, resourceful businessmen, stubborn caretakers, with iron muscles, and nerves of steel" (ibid., 286).

What Gladkov found in the end was a heightened value of "the romance of fierce battle." The final scene of Gleb's triumph at the official opening of the plant reveals Gladkov's newly found conviction about the saving strength of the passion of Christ.

Once there were deadly nights and days of battles, and he trembled for his life and kept thinking about Dasha. How far and removed they are now! Dasha . . . she is no more . . . does it really matter? All this is past and forgotten.
    And his old self is no longer there.There is that unbound enthusiasm and heart bursting with joy. Working class, republic, the great reconstruction. We know how to suffer, but we know how to enjoy, too! (ibid., 366)

These exclamations comprise the basic tenets of the New Christians. Gleb is awash in the feeling that he has fulfilled his work, that he has purged his life of the past and present through suffering and self-sacrifice.

Gladkov's ambivalence toward rationality echoes with Tolstoy's and Andreev's misgivings about the veneration of science and technology in the age of modernization. It is first of all a matter of emphasis. Gladkov centers on the relationships between man and machine, and between man and society. In Gleb's mournful wanderings about the plant, we are invited to watch, bemused, how the hymn to the machine and to human rationality degenerates into a lonely tune of human wretchedness and misery. If Gleb is disgusted by the workers' giving up on restoring the plant, he is by no means inspired by a worker absorbed with machines.

It is in the sparkling clean machine shop, "a temple" among the surrounding chaos and abomination of desolation, that Gladkov's perception of work is put to the test. His sympathies are torn between his admiration for perseverance and devotion to work and his sense of social participation. Gladkov's novel can be read as an endorsement of passion for the machine and, at the same time, as an assault upon the dehumanizing effect of rationality embodied in the machine. It presents a Marxist idea, modified by a Russian theme. The machine shop is described as "a temple, full of heavenly light," and "the idols," the diesel engines, embellished with "black marble, glitter and silver" (ibid., 24), are represented as surrealistically animated by some inner vigor--"push them and they will dance and sparkle." The hymn to technology and the machine is undermined and toned down by a gentle hint that when people erect temples and put idols on the altars, the "altars demand a sacrifice." It is man's love for his work and for machines that turns him into a social pariah. Gladkov feels that when man celebrates his final identification with a machine and shuns social participation, when he claims that "politics, bawling, and fighting is no concern of [his]" (ibid., 25), then the dehumanization process is complete. "The man stayed with the machines and his life stopped when the machine stopped. He was as lonely as those stern polished machines" (ibid., 26).

Gladkov's strong preoccupation with the spirituality of physical work perhaps reflected his childhood experience of growing up in a family of Old Believers (Alexandrova 1963, 34). For Gladkov, spirituality became a synonym of the socially useful, and was a favorite means of perpetuating the conflict between the forces of new and old, good and evil, loyalty and betrayal. Despite harsh chiaroscuro and valiant attempts to preserve the conflict, Gladkov's ambiguity reveals itself in Gleb's confrontation with the factory workers. The confrontation--the bathos of altruism debased by the social reality of the human need for food-- questions Bukharin's insistence that work should be driven by class struggle and class consciousness. Gleb's agony is palpable when he lashes out at the workers who "turned the plant into a filthy dump" while he and the others were "spilling their blood in the front, defending them" (Gladkov 1931, 34). It is the agony of a person appalled by the workers shortsighted indifference to the plant, the source of their livelihood and well-being. Gleb's blasting criticism of the workers and passionate insistence on self-sacrifice are critically undermined when he requests food stamps and a bread card.[8] It might well be that Gladkov, writing his novels in a squalid kennel-like basement, starving and without food stamps and money,[9] realized that his work was not only the expression of his inspiration, but also the means of his survival. Thus the clash between Gleb and the workers is more than a drama of collision. It can also be seen as a drama of Gladkov's growing realization that work, besides being a passion, also means mundane survival and that while the spiritual part may dominate, purely human needs can no longer be ignored and people do need something "in return."

It is within the context of the depth of human tragedy and against the exuberant vitality of nature, with its inherent promise of hope, that we can better understand Gladkov's perplexity and ire, and his fervent belief in salvation. For as if to defy the somber reality of the starving children inhabiting the orphanage where Gleb and Dasha visit their daughter, Gladkov rhapsodizes about the surrounding landscape, the sea "boiling with glaring flickers, and the bees flying like stars" (ibid., 46). The paradox is only too obvious. The bony faces of the orphans against the vibrant colors of triumphant nature merge into a discordant celebration of "great human labor," which is incongruously animated by some "inner tremors of a stubborn gigantic work" (ibid., 47).

The literary superiority of the scene of the orphans "scavenging for some morsels, casting greedy furtive glances" is a mark of Gladkov's genuine talent; the pictures that he could so vividly bring into being were the pictures of violence and human misery. It is this human misery, and particularly children's misery, which we may recognize as the place of Gladkov's spiritual crisis, a hell of suffering where moral conscience is crystallized.

This is the world of Dasha, where human life is fraught with misery and violence from which no one, not even her only child, can be shielded. Once she was a gentle, loving wife and mother, but the core of her character has undergone a radical change as the result of a horrifying experience. Dasha was tortured and raped by the Whites, witnessed the execution of her friends, and escaped death only by a miracle. She dragged herself back to life, and when the Reds returned, immersed herself in work, supervising the orphanages and creches. But the scar of the deep psychological wound seems to have cut her off from all emotional attachments, even to her daughter. She watches as her daughter longs for motherly love and attention, but finds herself incapable of response. It is this tragedy of suppressed humanity, that mirrors Gladkov's wrenching concern about the newly emergent communist ethic of work. The following conversation bears witness to his pain.

"We, Dasha, are close only in work. As humans, we are aloof, we are complete strangers. We are only workers. And we are afraid of nothing lest we betray our feelings, the majority suffer from loneliness," complains Dasha's co-worker.
And Dasha replies, "You speak like a tender-hearted lady, Comrade Mekhova. It is true, we do not have the time for heart-to-heart talks. People can wait, but business, if you let it slip between your fingers, won't" (ibid., 189).

The air gets thicker and suffocating with Dasha's embittered suspicion of pervasive betrayal and treachery: "those damned women who are ready to plunder everybody and everything, the slaves . . . everybody, even our own proletarian kin, are the enemy" (ibid., 54). Dasha's paranoid fears of betrayal echo Lenin's fears and encapsulate the mood of the era of promise. In Dasha we discover the New Communist Woman, firmly set to liberate herself from all signs of dominance. Although she has her counterpart in other European fiction of the time Dasha nonetheless, is uniquely Russian insofar as she is presented as the epitome of universal salvation. Indeed, when she and Gleb visit their little daughter in the orphanage, Dasha seems almost inhuman when she coldly brushes off Gleb's indignant accusation that her indifference made their daughter scavenge for food at the dump with the other orphans. The snapshots of Dasha sparring with the thieving managers and the orphanage personnel bring to the fore a fiercely independent figure of a woman determined not to let anything or anybody impede on her lonely heroic crusade.

Dasha's path to rebirth is colored by her intimate acquaintance with harrowing experience. Gleb's road to redemption represents the psychological travail of a person suddenly jolted into the realization that "the life he has returned to has to be conquered" (ibid.,50). To be initiated into this new world, he has to combat the present. In the figures of Dasha and Gleb, Gladkov implied, almost against his own will, that the communist work ethic can be achieved only by total sacrifice of one's humanity, when a person's devotion to public duty destroys his or her private life.

Gladkov agonizes over Dasha's lack of response to her daughter. The suggestion that Dasha is a victim of some unintelligible force "which emanates from somewhere outside, from life, and keeps her in tight grip" (ibid., 294), reveals the ironic recurrence of the native sense of surrender. Gladkov feels that Dasha is not responsible for her own life and work. With the sense of responsibility removed, what is left then is "revolution, fight, work, party," and the self-effacing feeling of universal destiny, where "death ceases to exist" and a human being is "a speck of dust" (ibid.).

If we abstract a meaning from this utterance, we find something significant pertaining to the Russian perception of work. Human activity was seen as driven by passion, unquestioning faith, and enthusiasm. Untarnished by human frailties and mundane desires, the ethic of work was animated by the perennial Russian yearning for the kingdom of heaven, the realm of absolute perfection. It was through the pursuit of perfection that the Russian writer articulated his, and his heroes', sense of man's relation with the world. This conviction reverberated in Kataev's *Time, Forward!* and Makarenko's *Pedagogical Poem*.

It was in the fervor of competitions, contests, and the celebration of creative labor that Kataev got around to reflecting on his personal experiences. He added his robust accent to the hopeful mood of the believers: "in a drop of rain he saw a garden" (Kataev, in *Sobranie Sochinenii* 1956, 350). Kataev's impressions and experiences of travel to construction sites and his year-long stay in Magnitogorsk erupted in the ebullient plot of *Time, Forward!* (1932). The story, which is narrated

in the spirit of a sporting event, is animated by the urgency of the day--
the breakneck speed of industrialization. Kataev recreates the hectic
atmosphere of a single day at a gigantic construction site in Magnitogorsk. The kaleidoscopic events are driven by the determination of the
shift engineer, Lev D. Morgulies, and his team to beat the world record
for concrete mixing. The superhuman effort of heroism and selflessness
is crowned by success. As a newspaper correspondent, Kataev was an
alert trend-spotter and an able purveyor of the hopeful beliefs of the day.

The opening scene--the sprawling construction site in the wilderness
of the Ural mountains--represents the linking together of the relation of
man to his present, to his state in nature, and to his transcendent being.
"The merciless war" waged between man and hostile nature, embodied
in "the raging winds" and "the slanted towers of sand storms, oversha-
dowing the sun" (ibid., 199), invokes a sense of apocalypse. Kataev's
New Christians and their holy war against nature are the Russian
metaphor of resurrection, the recurring refraction of Vrubel's *Demon*
rebelling against God. Like St. Paul, who celebrated the passion of
Christ and his rebirth as "the New Man" after his death as "the Natural
Man," Kataev celebrates human victory over "the Natural Man's"
bondage to the forces of nature.

But Kataev, the troubadour of the New Christians and the myth-maker
of the communist work ethic, could but feel ambivalent about the benefits
of modernization. It is instructive that Kataev's reservations are voiced
by an American concessionaire whose brief appearance in the story takes
place away from the "hell" of the construction site. The oscillation
between the scenes of chaos and human ineptitude at the building site and
the glorious scenes of the harmonious and serene beauty of nature betray
with unusual force the author's doubts. The American is shown around
by the chief engineer, Nalbadnov, who is the epitome of rationalized
caution and a staunch opponent of Morgulies's drive to set a record. The
conversation between the American and the Russian swarms with
gnawing doubts about man's quarrel with nature and with muffled
innuendos and challenges. The American looks round in dismay at what
was once "a tiny steppe river" that has become a "brand new" (ibid.,
366) lake created to meet the needs of the future industrial giant. He
observes wistfully man's failure to reorder the natural order of things:
"Your geometry has failed God's test. You wanted to create a full size
lake, but managed to create only a half" (ibid., 367). But the Russian
points out that it was not a lake they were after, but a reservoir of
industrial water, and, therefore, they do control nature. The moral
follows, the ode to human suffering and self-sacrifice. The Russian says:

The work on laying down concrete was carried out at forty degrees
below zero, under hellish winds. The water for the concrete had to be
warmed. People, their feet and hands injured by frostbite, kept on
working. The work was beyond human endurance but it went on. It
was a battle between man and nature. And man claimed the victory
(ibid.).

Many things are being tested as well as exemplified in this conversation. First is the American's celebration of "the Natural Man" in
harmony with nature. Second is the Russian's defense of the "New Man"
who seeks to control the elements. Another of the things challenged by
Kataev here is the traditional Russian reverence for and surrender to the
forces of nature. Among them, too, is the proposition, implicit in
Tolstoy, Vrubel, Gorky, and Andreev, that the value of work is to be
found in man's challenge to the present, to the sociopolitical reality. If
the present still poses a challenge, its nature, for Kataev, is defined by
the Soviet drive for modernization and the demand for self-sacrifice.

The American, having heard the Russian's proud saga of a heroism
and self-sacrifice in building the dam, observes pensively:

Fingers frost-bitten, people ready to drop from cold and fatigue, a crazy duel of man with god. And here--a kilometer-long dam. And a half
-size lake. Man thinks he's conquered nature. Man celebrates. But why
does man need all that? Water for industry. Wonderful. Why does he
need industry? To create things. Wonderful. But why would he need
things? Are they needed for happiness? Youth and health--that is all
that is needed for happiness.

Look, Comrade Nalbadnov, we have moved some eight kilometers
away from this hell and how beautiful is the change! How wonderful-
ly warm is the breath of nature! How soothing is the primeval silence!
Hardly had we left the technology, than we came closer to god (ibid.,
367-8).

And the Russian challenges the American with hard-nosed reality: "Sure,
. . . closer to god by the latest model car" (ibid., 368).
The subject of these utterances, bristling with native passion and moral
alertness, introduces, as Kataev sees it, two vexingly contradictory
positions: on the one hand, a passion, an obsession, which, granted the
tough nature of reality, must be a proof of spiritual courage and tenacity
of belief; on the other, a pervasive sense of a paradise lost, a dawning
realization that the act of sacrifice and the yearning for happiness have
been defiled by a search for material ends. The final touch--the latest

model car to provide access to man's communion with nature--sounds ironic and irrelevant.

It is Kataev, conveniently hiding behind the American's eloquence, who betrays the wrenching pain of contradictory feelings in a dire warning of impending catastrophe: "You know the fate of Herculaneum and Pompeii? Wonderful! Sometimes nature loses its patience. Then it buries its rebellious children under boiling lava" (ibid., 371). To canvass the present exhaustively, in order to show that human happiness transcends mundane reality and has no link to it is a curious twist in the narrative and very Russian.

These contradictions have affinities with the contemporary moral visions of the ardent believers and gloomy pessimists. If Kataev grasped them and brushed upon them, however slightly, it was because his newly found belief in modernization still quarreled with the old native image, which was hostile to the pursuit of material well-being. But when Kataev glanced back and stumbled, he immediately steadied himself and moved resolutely, like Gladkov before him, to the unambiguous light of a newly found hope.

Kataev's profound value is a hope in universal salvation. According to him, "revolution will come to the West" (ibid., 204), and the New Communist Man, unlike the Westerner, who is enslaved by nature and tradition, is God, and nature yields to his creative powers. This conjunction of slavery and freedom, of the Natural Man and the New Man, is at the heart of the meeting of the Soviet and the Western perceptions of work.

It is highly significant that Kataev, like Gladkov before him, uses a non-Russian, Morgulies (whose given names, Lev Davidovich are clearly non-Russian), to energize the process of work with Western efficiency and rationality. Ironically, Kataev's desire to celebrate efficiency and rationality in work is modified by the Russian value of spirituality. Morgulies's devotion to efficiency is determined not by a mechanical device, such as a wristwatch, but by his almost intimate *feeling* for time. Time and speed are symbolized by the wristwatch--not by its presence but by the acknowledgment of its absence. Morgulies hence becomes the symbol of the New Man redefining time within the paradigm of work. Time is "the number of revolutions of a drum; the beginning or the end of the shift; the quality of cement" (ibid., 402). What we have here then is more than a New Man redefining the world through his work. It is the transfiguration of the Russian yearning for the freedom of will and a belief in the miracles of science that will finally release man the from earthly bonds of nature, "when man will reach the speed of light and will become immortal" (ibid., 344).

For Kataev, the central tension in Soviet reality was dramatic. The pounding noise of the train, rushing from west to east, to Magnitogorsk, echoes the pounding sounds of Stalin's speech, bursting from the pages of the newspaper. Kataev's sense of drama intertwines the frenzied speed of the train with Stalin's call for increased tempo and the fleeting outlines of the giant construction sites behind the windows with his dire warning of possible defeat lest the speed is increased: "to slacken the tempo means to fall behind. And the backward are always beaten. But we do not want to be beaten! The story of old Russia was the story of its constant defeat for its backwardness . . . military, cultural, state, industrial, and agricultural" (ibid., 205).[10] This vision is the frame, the burden of the dialectic movement in the newly defined work ethic. It, Kataev cheerfully insists, would "create" its own history for "the cement-mixing machine, the witness of the world-breaking record is no less important than the rusty guillotine" (ibid., 516).

The conclusion effected in the story has to do with the message forced upon the reader of the absolute value of the heroic deed of self-sacrifice. The image of a heroic personality is conjured by carefully detailing the pain of privation and the human effort which raises him to the Christlike pinnacle of heroism. It is the heroic deed alone that paves the road to salvation.

But it was Anton Makarenko (1889-1939) who most closely identified with Christlike heroism and who exploited the myth and reality of the passion of Christ in the dingy world of Soviet reform institution.

> I expected neither mercy nor leniency. In the tall huge hall I faced, at last, the whole assembly of the prophets and the angels. It was . . . a Sanhedrin, no less. (Makarenko, *The Pedagogical Poem*)

Kataev's story was perfectly designed to celebrate the New Christians shaping their own redemption and to sustain the Russian's most durable image. But it was Makarenko's *The Pedagogical Poem* (1925-1935) that commented with irony and wit on the treacherous and bumpy road to creating New Man. In Russian culture, where concern for social justice is an integral part of the literary tradition, the durability of the passion of Christ owes as much to Makarenko, a professional educator, as to the masters of Russian letters.

More than a decade before Kataev began *Time, Forward!* Makarenko agreed to take on the leadership of a colony for juvenile delinquents. *The Pedagogical Poem* was his real-life tale of the almost inhuman self-sacrifice, heroic passion, and final redemption of most of his pupils. Makarenko's book about his work in the colony laid the cornerstone for the Soviet method of socializing young people through education in the communist work ethic. The dialectic of passion and redemption--the central drama of the Russian life and letters--was the special and sensitive means by which Makarenko gauged the moral stamina of the people with whom he was working, as well as the moral mood of the life he described in *The Pedagogical Poem.*

Although there were many facets to Makarenko's personality, it was his belief in the passion of Christ mythology that is of particular interest here. Makarenko saw himself in relation to the contemporary Soviet pedagogical establishment as Jesus Christ on trial before "the whole Council" (the Sanhedrin), as the indomitable mover and savior, mocked and condemned, who is redeemed in the New Men he brought into the social fray from the dingy world of crime and homelessness.

The longer Makarenko wrote *The Pedagogical Poem*, the closer he moved from the romantic manner of representation of the early Maxim Gorky toward blending the native anecdote with Western rationalism. His treatment was similar to that of Kataev; it was a realistic chronicle of concrete social events. Unlike Kataev, Makarenko, who was a man of adamant will and uncontrollable passions, did not live vicariously, but was a direct participant in the evolutionary drama of redemption.

Makarenko brought to his subject of education a prose style distinguished by wry wit and the exuberant fervor of revolutionary romanticism, which included a robust faith in the power of the passion of Christ. Makarenko was the Gorky of the educators, the best writer among them. As for his style, it is overpowering. Makarenko's domineering spirit, a key aspect of his personality, very likely represented a desire to suppress his feeble physical presence. Bolding, thin, and bespectacled, Makarenko seemed to compensate for his frail looks with his zest for challenge and overcoming obstacles. "The insanity of the brave we hail in songs" (ibid., 330) represented Makarenko's inner sense of drama and reckless heroism in accepting the task of "making" New Men out of the inhabitants of a "bandit nest" (ibid., 334) whose way of life was gangsterism and theft.

Makarenko was a dramatizer to the core. He lived and worked on the edge of a pedagogical precipice, looking into the void, which echoed his frustration and despair. "So many books, so much paper, so much glory . . . and so totally mute about dealing with the offenders, no method, no tools, no logic" (ibid., 86-87). The whole of Makarenko's *Poem*, over five hundred pages, is an account of heroic assaults on the curse of the present. It is Makarenko's assault of the will upon indolence and upon the native anarchy of the spirit and his personal assault on the pedagogical establishment. In the social reality of Russia, which moved away from the revolutionary fervor of the heroic deed to a detached rationality of labor ethics, Makarenko endowed his concept of labor discipline with an ardent belief in the passion of Christ. It is within this paradigm that we can understand Makarenko's vision of communist work and its relationship to the passion of Christ.

As the story of the youth labor colony unfolds, Makarenko, flanked by two "heroic" female teachers and a bursar, takes his first tentative steps towards reforming in "new, labor-active life" (ibid., 13) six teenage criminals, whose charges range from armed robbery to theft. The environment with its "deserted forest, surrounding the colony;" "ten benches instead of beds; an ax and a spade for the instruments;" and its "long, dread-filled winter nights" (ibid., 14-15), is animated by a conflict brewing between the adults and the pupils. Attempts to reason with the colonists to do some work around the colony are rebuffed by insolent mockery. The air dangerously darkens and thickens with the colonists openly threatening the adults while "demonstratively playing with the Finnish knives" (ibid., 16).

The tenuous silent torment erupts into violence and a resounding victory for Makarenko. Brought to the end of his tether by the colonists' insolence and mockery, Makarenko beats up the tormentor who refuses to do his share of the work around the colony. The rupture signals more than a revolt against the pedagogical theory of the day, "a loss of balance on the pedagogical rope" (ibid., 16); it breaks the status quo. The teachers reconcile themselves to doing the work around the colony, while the pupils rob the people on the highway and return to the colony for the night. Makarenko's control is affirmed. Dourly amused by the pupils' sudden docility and open admiration of his prowess, Makarenko gets the first inkling of the power of heroism and self-sacrificial work:

Zadorov [the colonist] is stronger than I am; he could have crippled me with one blow. He is not afraid of anything, none of them are. In this whole incident they see not the thrashing, but anger, human explosion. They understand perfectly well that I could have done without the thrashing, I could have sent him back [to prison]. But I have not done it. I have committed this human, but by no means formal, deed. Moreover, they see how hard we work for their sake. . . . And it is a very important circumstance (ibid., 19).

It is within this paradigm of the rupture between the rationality of scholastic pedagogy and the irrationality of raw human feeling that a decisive change in the behavior of the colonists takes place. With relish and self-righteous pride Makarenko relates how on another occasion he again lets passion overtake the impartiality of pedagogical rationality.

When the perpetrator of physical abuse defies his orders prohibiting the harassment of other pupils, Makarenko gives vent to his anger: "the pedagogical foundation came crushing down under my feet. The heavy abacus, lying on my table went flying at Osadchii's head. I missed" (ibid., 83).

What lies behind the eruption is the firm inner belief in the value of the absolute. Violence is perceived as a remedy against violence. The violence of passion is rectified by the strength of Makarenko's commitment to the well-being of his colony. Anticipating the peda- gogues' indignation and outdistancing them at their own game, Makarenko hastens to point out the salubrious "sense of humanism" and "the healthy and enthusiastic rhythm" (ibid., 86) that set in among the colonists after the incident. Makarenko's choice of dramatic metaphors-- the "loss of balance on the pedagogical rope," the "pedagogical foundation came crushing down"-- demonstrates his dislike of rational theory, "the technology of education" (ibid.). "Technology" is unable to provide proper guidance, "no method, no logic, nothing. Real charlatan- ism"(ibid., 87).

Throughout the narrative, Makarenko insists that the work of a pedagogue is something more than rational theory. It is his root princi- ple, his position, and his doctrine that work is a deed exercised in the center of a life of a group, a matter--in Makarenko's favorite expression --of *podvizhnechestvo* (heroic selfless devotion). In coming to this posi- tion, Makarenko drew upon the Bolsheviks' vision of the communist ethic of work. He also gave the process of socialization a traditional folk flavor, a blend of religious ritual and military discipline. Makarenko felt that inasmuch as the survival of the colony depended on his pupils' productive work, the pupils needed the inspiration of a religious ritual and the rigor of discipline to perform it. It was ritual and discipline which animated and sustained the heroic deed. When Makarenko scrutinized the notion of work stripped of heroic drive and readiness for self-sacrifice, he saw in it, like the Russian peasant did, only suffering and pain.

If one looks upon the notion of work soberly, one has to recognize that there are many kinds of work which are hard, unpleasant, uninterest- ing; many kinds of work require a lot of patience, a habit to withstand painful depressing sensations in the body; many kinds of work are pos- sible only because man has been taught to suffer and endure" (ibid., 465).

The revealing emphasis on "suffering" and "endurance" in work is almost a pastiche of Tolstoy's celebration of altruistic labor--suffering and endurance for the sake of the other. Not only did Makarenko, like Tolstoy, celebrate labor, he also named the beneficiary--the collective--of the individual's heroic deed and self-sacrifice.

> One can't build the whole process of education on interest alone. I required bringing up a physically strong person, who could do any unpleasant and boring work if it were required by the needs of the collective. I demanded the creation of a strong, severe, if necessary, enthusiastic collective. All my hopes were in the collective" (ibid., 104).

The identifiers established here tell us a good deal. Using "severe" and "strong," Makarenko seems to echo the biblical description of god. "Enthusiastic" is a correlative of the believer, the disciple. Thus the combination of the identifiers implies the religious entity of god and believer coalesced into one. Here Makarenko arrives at his dedication to the "strong," "severe," and "enthusiastic collective" not out of an ardent passion but out of a hard, uncompromising, and sternly masculine ideal of work subordinating the individual to the interests of collective. Makarenko asserts that the interests of the collective can justify coercion if passion and readiness for self-sacrifice are missing. "If there is no collective and its representative bodies, if there is no tradition and no elementary labor and life-experience skills, an educator has the right and must resort to coercion" (ibid.).

The pathos of a military ceremony preceding the work in the field sets the tone for the colonists' baptism in the "suffering and endurance" of agricultural work.

> The fourth composite detachment works around the clock. . . . At four o'clock in the morning, that is already after the breakfast, the fourth detachment lines up across from the main entrance. On the right flank of the row line up the educators. They, as a matter of fact, don't have to participate in the work, except for two duties to which they have been assigned. Nonetheless, it's an honor to work in the fourth detachment. No self-respecting person'd miss the order to set up the fourth composite detachment.
>
> Eight drummers run out, rattling on their drums; four trumpeters march out and stand at attention. All hands are risen in salute. The girl on duty, in her best dress, with a red hand-band, carries the silk Gorky banner, flanked by two coldly alert bayonets, accompanied by the

raucous noise of the drums and the silvery greetings of the trumpets. The drumming march brings everybody to his place. The fourth composite detachment sets out to work in the field (ibid., 319).

The choice of vocabulary-- "detachment," "flank," "on duty," "order"-- reveal the masculine, military precision and "iron" discipline, as perceived by Makarenko. Makarenko's world was a world of unending "dialectics" of "fights" (ibid.). Resisting the encroachment of "philistinism" would have been, Makarenko appears to suggest, an act of personal and universal salvation.

Makarenko's redemption was that of a fierce savior bent relentlessly on his course. The mission of this work-affirming Soviet Christ was to educate his readers in the religion of work by means that were familiar to the Russian religious believer: the adulation of suffering and self-sacrifice. Makarenko subjected the substance of work to radical critique in order to see what remained of it when "suffering and self-sacrifice," the qualities identifying a heroic deed, were removed from the human condition. What he found and recoiled from in disgust was "the boring concern about one's future earnings, the much-vaunted qualification. And what qualification are they talking about? Shoemaker, carpenter, miller" (ibid.). Makarenko insists, like Tolstoy, Gorky and Andreev before him, that "the highest qualification for a sixteen-year-old is the qualification of a fighter and a man" (ibid.). There should be no doubt, however, that the passion of Christ mythology was Makarenko's first and foremost powerful driving perception, the formula for redeeming the world, which he contemplated in his *Poem*. Makarenko was occupied primarily with the process of redemption of young criminals and socializing them in the ethics of work. The New Man was to be "forged" (ibid., 13) in socially useful work; the concept was celebrated in the functional name of the colony, *trudovaia-vospitatel'naia* (labor-educational).

Makarenko's saw himself as a heroic personality who gave "a good portion of his own life" (ibid., 325) to transform "knife-happy" criminals into highly skilled professionals. Makarenko replaced the contemporary vision of the passion of Christ with his own stern and militant savior. *The Pedagogical Poem*, Makarenko's thorough rendering of salvation, charted a road to creating a New Communist Man. Inasmuch as this road was fraught with violence and hope, it provided a powerful commentary on the tenacity of the passion of Christ and its redemptive powers. But there were other commentaries whose themes of the passion of Christ and human work provided comparable challenges to inquiry and keys to understanding the Russian and his concept of work.

8

The Irony of the Deed:
Olesha and Pil'niak

The New Christians' celebration of the communist work ethic--the militant masculinity of the collective-oriented heroic deed--was soured by the apocalyptic voices of skepticism and vehement repudiation. In the chorus of skeptics and critics, the most eloquent voices belonged to Iurii Olesha (1899-1960) and Boris Pil'niak, which was the pseudonym of Vogau (1894-1937?). The accent on militant masculinity--the spirit tamed by the rigors of reason and discipline--seemed to Olesha and Pil'niak like a mocking violation of what the native image held dear--the freedom of will and the value of the irrational.

Olesha, who was born into a middle-class family, like Gladkov, joined the Red Army in 1919 and was assigned to work as a journalist-propagandist (Terras 1991, 575). Like Kataev, he moved to Moscow in the 1920s to write for the railway workers' newspaper *Gudok* (Russel 1981, 17). Unlike Gladkov and Kataev, however, Olesha felt at odds with the Bolsheviks' vision of rationality and efficiency. Olesha was convinced, as Pil'niak was, that the Bolsheviks' drive for rationality was destructive to creative work, individuality, and human feelings. In *Envy*, written in 1927, during the NEP, Olesha's inner turmoil and anguish erupted in the surrealistic tale of two brothers, representatives of the two Russias, the old and the new.

If Olesha's *Envy* catapulted him to instant fame (Alexandrova 1963, 162), Pil'niak's *Mahogany,* written in 1929, during the First Five Year Plan, became the subject of vicious attacks in the Soviet press for its allegedly Trotskyist sympathies.[1] Pil'niak, the son of a veterinarian in the province of Moscow, was a leading Soviet writer by the time he wrote *Mahogany* and, according to V. A. Terras, enjoyed excellent relations with the Kremlin in the early 1920s. However, with the publication of *The Tale of Unextinguished Moon* (1926), in which Pil'niak alluded to Stalin's plot to murder Mikhil Frunze, a popular Red Army commander (Terras 1991, 569-70), and with Stalin's final victory for power in 1928, Pil'niak felt under siege. *Mahogany*, an intricate arabesque of episodes, gives voice to Pil'niak's torment and despair about the vanishing values of human passion and the deed of suffering and self-sacrifice.

Anecdotes abstracted from Olesha's *Envy* and Pil'niak's *Mahogany* reveal in the clinging clashes of absolutes--of a free will and discipline, the irrational and the rational, the individual and the collective--the tragic irony of the heroic deed in a modernizing society. It was Iurii Olesha who detected and responded with irony and wit to the Soviet version of the passion of Christ.

Envy is electrified more by the author's sense of envy and resentment toward the believers in the age of revolution than by the plot, which is hardly present. The bathos of clash between the traditional, "the banal," and the new, "the revolutionary," is manifested in the grotesque encounters between the two brothers, Ivan, a former engineer and a hard drinker, and Andrei Babichev, a respected Soviet functionary and the director of a food trust. The conflict branches off into the rivulets of ironic collisions between the younger generation, represented by Nikolai Kavalerov, who, according to Olesha himself, "looks at the world with my eyes," (Olesha, "Speech . . ," in *Zavist'* 1973, 235) and Andrei's disciple, Volodia Makarov.

Andrei Babichev, the epitome of efficiency, rationality, and hard work, plans to build a giant food trust, which would relieve a housewife from her "slavery in the kitchen." His pet project is called *chetvertak* (quarter), which means that a meal there would cost a pittance, a quarter. An old Bolshevik, Andrei wears the marks of bullet scars, the reminders of his past revolutionary glory.

For Olesha, the central strain in the emerging stress on rationality is ironic. Olesha's laughter denies and asserts, condemns and celebrates; it is the sardonic laughter of a victim who painfully realizes his impotence. Olesha's fury of disenchantment is voiced in the tone and rhythm of a narrative heightened by the dexterous manipulation of metaphors, which merge the spiritual and the base, the old and the new, the irrational and the rational, and the feminine and the masculine in burlesque tragico-mical unity. Olesha's sense of raging envy and impotence rips the vision of "the room full of air, light, and radiance," to expose the base--Andrei Babichev's groin, covered by his underwear, while he goes through the routine of his morning calisthenics. The visual imagery of Babichev's groin, succinctly outlined in a string of metaphors--"a tender scorch-mark, a reclusive nook, the groin of a stud. This very chamois matte groin I saw on a male antelope. Girls love him" (Olesha 1973, 14)--is intertwined with the explicit trope of bestiality: when he eats "his eyes become bloodshot, he chomps, breathes heavily through his nose, his ears move" (ibid., 15). Olesha's mockery and scorn are pervasive and they extinguish whatever spark of respect the reader might have felt for Andrei Babichev, "one of the most outstanding people in the state" (ibid.). The image of Andrei Babichev, a hard working, efficient, and rational director, is overshadowed and eradicated by Olesha's emphasis on Andrei Babichev's masculinity, reproductive prowess, and greed.

Andrei's young disciple, Volodia Makarov, once saved his life, and the grateful Babichev adopted him. Volodia Makarov, everybody's object of love and respect, is impeccably groomed by his benefactor to become the best image of the New Man. Unlike Andrei, who is prone to irrational fits of kindness--for instance, in a fit of compassion, he picked up Kavalerov, a perfect stranger, lying in the street, drunk, and brought him into his apartment--Volodia is not given to sentimental weakness. Volodia believes that Andrei's sentimental irrationality stems from the nature of his work with food, "fruit, gentle grass, tiny bees, and gentle calves." Volodia, "a man of industry, a new generation" (ibid., 44), has subjected all his feelings to calculating rationality. Far from being swept off his feet by love, he has planned assiduously the place and occasion for the first kiss between him and his fiancee Valia, who is Andrei's niece and Ivan's daughter. The kiss with Valia, whom Volodia has been dating for four years, will take place on the podium, with the band playing, during the ceremonies celebrating the opening of Andrei's *chetvertak*. Olesha's irony is larger than life; it is almost tangible.

Both Olesha and his hero, Nikolai Kavalerov, who is installed in Andrei Babichev's apartment, feel that in this brand new world of machinery and rationality, of the New Man and the new values, a person anchored in the traditional values of human sentiments and passions is out of place. This person from the old world is perceived as mentally sick, as someone who should be placed in a mental institution, "so he would stop imagining things" (ibid., 47).

Kavalerov is close in spirit to Andrei's brother, Ivan, whom he first observes in the street. Ivan Babichev, a jolly, pudgy little fellow in an outlandish bowler hat, dragging a huge pillow, is unsuccessfully trying to see his daughter Valia, who feels ashamed of her weird looking father and refuses to talk to him. Kavalerov discovers, to his amazement and delight, that Ivan is Andrei's brother and his bitter foe. Ivan, who earns his living by performing card tricks, "sketching portraits, improvisations, [and] palm reading" (ibid., 56), dreams of destroying his brother Andrei, who he believes has turned his daughter Valia against him. Ivan visualizes the destruction of Andrei's new mechanized society by a machine with a symbolic name--Ophelia. This new modernizing society and its New Men, Ivan insists, have killed his daughter's ability to love him, and this new world has made his brother Andrei his enemy. In Ivan's dream, the machine, whose name, Ophelia, echoes the tragedy of "a young girl who lost her mind from love and despair" (ibid., 73), will wreak revenge on this mechanistic, rational society. This machine, "the greatest creation of technology," will be incapacitated by its ability to have human feelings. "She, the machine that can do everything," Ivan rejoices, "will deprive humanity of its superior help" and instead "will sing the sentimental songs of the past age, and it will pick flowers" (ibid.). Ivan, like Olesha, refuses to participate in this new life and loathes its emphasis on rationality.

Ivan Babichev is Jesus Christ reincarnated, but for Olesha, the image of Ivan the Christ is unmistakably ironic. The irony is attributed to Ivan, the savior, and to his potential disciples, "the actors, dreaming about fame, the wretched lovers, the spinsters, the bookkeepers, the ambitious, the fools, the knights, and the cowards" (ibid., 57). Olesha's irony is insidious, especially in the order in which the disciples are assembled. "The knights" precede "the cowards;" the boisterous and robust "ambitious" are in the close company of the "fools" and the bland; and colorless "bookkeepers" deride and debase the retinue and the "prophet."

Olesha's ambivalence about the value of the passion of Christ in this emergent rational social order is revealed in his joking collusion of the two images of Ivan. One is Ivan the preacher and the prophet; the other is Ivan the clumsy drunk, "climbing on the table, kicking the heads, snatching at the palm leaves, breaking the bottles, toppling the potted palmtree" (ibid., 57). The oscillation between the noble and the base, the spirit and the body, betrays with unusual force Olesha's ambiguity toward Ivan Babichev. Let us look closely at Ivan the preacher. Ivan Babichev delivered a sermon.

We are the humanity which has reached its limit. Strong personalities, the people who have decided to follow their own route, the egoists, the stubborn, you are the ones I am turning to. . . . Listen you, standing at the forefront! The epoch is coming to an end. A billow is breaking against the stones: the billow is on the boil, the froth is glistening.

And what do you want? What? To vanish, to turn into nothing like those drops of water, plain boiling water? . . . the gates are closing. Do not try to get inside! Stop there! To stop is to show pride. Be proud. I am your leader, I am the king of the banal. All those who sing and plow the table with their nose when all the beer's been drunk up and are refused to be served more--those should be here, next to me. Come ye, burdened by grief, carried by song. You who murder out of jealousy and you who tie your own noose--I call you all, the children of the dying era: come ye, the banal and the dreamers, the fathers of families, doting on their daughters, the honest philistines, the people devoted to tradition, obeying the norms of honor, duty, and love, who are afraid of blood and riots, my dear soldiers and generals, let's march on!

Where? I'll direct you (ibid., 56-57).

So Ivan Babichev addresses a pub habitué. The above speech is in part a parody of the opening theme of the teaching and preaching of Jesus, who declared that "the time is fulfilled, and the kingdom of God is at hand" (Mark 1:15, in Brownrigg 1980, 173).

The comic parallelism between Ivan Babichev and Jesus is evident in Olesha's hilarious account of the rumors going around about Ivan the preacher, who performs miracles and is able to float.[2] According to one of the rumors, Ivan the preacher goes around issuing warnings. Unlike the traditional Christ, however, Ivan preaches disharmony and war. "Do not love each other," Ivan appeals to the newlyweds, "Do not unite. Groom, leave the bride! What will be the fruit of your love? You will reproduce your own enemy. He will devour you." The inversion becomes complete, when "the wine [at the wedding] turns into the water" (Olesha 1973, 59). According to another rumor, Ivan, who sees his brother Andrei in a car rolling along a very noisy street, "takes up his stand in the middle of the road, his hands wide spread, like that of a scarecrow" (ibid., 59) and blocks the way. Then, thronged by an admiring crowd, Ivan miraculously is lifted up in the air and floats over the heads of his supporters, "tumbling, rolling, jerking. His bowler hat slides back, revealing the broad serene forehead of a tired man" (ibid., 60).

The visual imagery of a comic bobbling body is ruptured and diminished by the ennobling effect of "a broad serene forehead of a tired man." This fleeing effect, however, is deftly extinguished by physical and psychological debasement: the floating prophet is downcast. Unlike Vrubel's the *Demon Downcast*, Ivan has no honor and glory left. Andrei grabs him by his pants and pulls him down. Ivan is carted off to the police station. Moreover, Olesha seems to strip his hero of any sense of dignity and respect. As it turns out, the encounter was, as Ivan calls it, "a folk legend," and the actual arrest took place in a pub, under more prosaic circumstances. Against this humiliating evidence, Olesha hurries to rescue his "prophet." He suggests that the garrulous, indolent Ivan

Babichev, who is an extravagant dreamer and visionary, has become the subject of folk legends because "in times of transition people yearn for a legend of courage and heroism" (ibid., 61).

I believe that Olesha felt more acutely than other of his contemporaries the irony of the heroic deed in a society preoccupied with rationality and material well-being. Although Ivan is a bubbling travesty of his brother Andrei, the noted revolutionary and rational and practical director of a famous food trust, it is Ivan, rather than his dull and tedious brother, who commands Olesha's attention. Ivan Babichev, Jesus with a pillow, is Olesha's ironic trope of the passion of Christ, debased and topographically reconstructed. The cosmic idea of universal salvation has been moved to the less glamorous and more earthly matter of human feelings. The pillow Ivan Babichev drags along is a metaphor for the family hearth and the feelings which Ivan fears are doomed to extinction by his brother Andrei and the Soviet state. In this new rational social order, human feelings are declared extinct, and the collective claims the individual's allegiance. Ivan Babichev envisions a tragic future where the ambitious food enterprise his brother is creating will destroy the family gathering at the kitchen table. It will lure people into cheap, efficient public canteens that are devoid of human feelings.

The raucous laughter ripping Ivan's fantasy of the destruction of the food enterprise is interspersed with the somber notes of apocalypse. The tragicomic deconstruction of the revolution is inferred in the conspicuous insistence on the preacher carrying a huge yellow pillow and the exaggerated emphasis on the object that debases and elevates, asserts and derides, destroys and redeems:

> The oddball came with a pillow. He carried a big pillow in a yellow pillowcase, worn out, privy to many heads sleeping on it . . . he stated ascending the stairs to the podium . . . a man from the presidium was supposed to stop him, but . . . his hand froze raised in the air. . . .
>
> It's hypnoses, somebody in the crowd screamed out. And the stanger kept climbing the stairs, dragging behind him the pillow. . . . And then the stranger spoke out:
>
> Friends! They want to take away your most dear thing: your hearth. The horses of the revolution, clanking on the backstairs, running over your children and your cats, your ceramic tiles and your bricks, will storm into your kitchens. Women, they threaten your pride and your glory--your hearth! The elephants of the revolution want to destroy your kitchen, mothers and wives! . . . they mock your pots and pans, your peace, your right to stick a pacifier into your child's mouth.

. . . They want you to forget your home . . . your native, dear home
. . . kick them out! Here is a pillow. I am the king of pillows. Tell
them: we want to sleep on our own pillows. Hands off our pillows!
Our heads, untouched by the down, rested on those pillows, our kisses
touched them accidentally in our nights of love, we died on them,
and those whom we killed died on them. . . . Do not entice us, do not
call us. What can you offer in exchange for our ability to love, hate,
pity, and to forgive? . . . Our emblem, our banner, our pillow. The
bullets get stuck in our pillow. We will smother you with the pillow
(ibid., 76-77).

In trying to grasp the meaning of the grotesque symbolism of the
above extract, it is clear that Olesha's strenuous doubts about the values
of the newly emergent ethics of industrial society, with its rationality and
collectivism, are embraced by a larger doubt which has to do with the
decreased value of the heroic deed in an industrial society. Olesha was
sure that a heroic deed was double; it was contained in the two polar
absolutes: a magnificent self-sacrifice and a glorious death, or complete
resignation and the apathy of surrender.

Olesha inserted this double-pronged solution into the novel. A
comparison of Ivan Babichev "on his Golgotha" (ibid., 67), voicing his
credo of glorious death to the police investigator, and Ivan Babichev at
the closing of the novel, ebulliently resigned in the face of total defeat,
yields an important glimpse into Olesha's perception of human activity
in an alien environment. Here is Ivan with the police investigator:

Take an electric bulb that has suddenly blacked out. It has burned out,
you say. But if you shake it up, it will flare up and will burn for quite
a while. A short, unrealistic, obviously doomed life--fever, too bright
a light, glitter. Then there is darkness, the life won't come back . . .
    But this short glitter is magnificent! I want to shake up the heart
of the burned out epoch. . . . I want to gather around me the multitude. To have a choice of the most brilliant, to make a shock group,
a group of feelings (ibid., 61-62).

The deceptive cadence of the language linking a material object, an
electric bulb, with the skillfully executed visual details of an instanta-
neous "flare up" carries the reader back into the larger-than-life tale of
heroic self-sacrifice, glorious death, and redemption.

But then there is Ivan sitting on a widow's ample bed, "the blanket
billowing around him like a cloud. He is gulping down red wine, and
scratching himself under the blanket" (ibid., 93). He is not in the least

concerned that he will share the widow and her bed with another loser like himself, for this is a matter of convenience, not love. It is not a home and hearth, but an arrangement, for he has found refuge in the newly discovered feeling that "indifference is the best condition of the human mind," and, therefore, he says to Kavalerov, his companion, "today is your turn to sleep with Anechka, hurrah!" (ibid., 93-94)

It is in the interplay, the so-to-speak open-ended dialectic of the two images of Ivan,--one "on Golgotha," the other in the widow's bed--that Olesha's relation to the heroic deed and self-sacrifice is to be found and where his pain and ambiguity reveal themselves. Ivan's plea for human passion in work is correlative to Olesha's plea for freedom to pursue his individual ambitions, unshackled by the demands of the collective. The bathos of Ivan's final surrender is the voice of the author who is painfully aware of his impotence and humiliating defeat. The final defeat of the traditional passionate deed by militant masculinity and reason is the ironic travesty of the contemporary voices of Chekhov and Tolstoy.

It was Olesha who, like Tolstoy and Gladkov, saw in the advent of the machine age the loss of humanism, the sacrifice of man to the Moloch of industrial production. Needless to say this was an affront to the official vision, for Olesha's comments on the ironic deed tell about the freedom of will and the courage needed to gain it and about its final loss and the author's valiant attempts to pose moral questions about human work. Olesha's Ivan Babichev suggests what might happen when the native image of the passion of Christ is pitted against the rational and the collective-minded ethic, when the conditions that alienated him from his surrounding have rendered him spiritually bankrupt.

> The alcohol frigate on the table was clearing Iakov Karpovich's thoughts like a northeast wind. A Russian Voltaire had been lodged in the mahogany of the parlor since the eighteenth century, along with the frigate. Outside the windows of this eighteenth century flowed a provincial Soviet night.
>
> Above the town the next morning the bells were dying, and they howled as they tore into tatters (Pil'niak 1965, 441).

If Olesha suspected a shift in the value of the heroic deed, Boris Pil'niak detected the somber ambiguity of the shift. And having done so, he ripped off from the Russian province the illusory veneer of change. The shift from Olesha's Ivan Babichev to Pil'niak's Ivan Ozhogov, who is an okhlomon[3] (a holy fool), is a process of embittering. The essential continuity between Gladkov, Kataev, Olesha, and Pil'niak explains itself through the geographical transformation whereby the native image of the passion of Christ receives different accents in the city and in the province. Unlike Gladkov, a native of Novorossiisk, a large seaport city, which was the prototype of the city in *The Cement,* and Kataev and Olesha, who grew up in Odessa, another large seaport city, and whose major characters are urbanites, Pil'niak grew up in the small provincial town of Mozhaisk, in the backwoods of the province of Moscow. Pil'niak's experience and knowledge stemmed from small provincial towns, where the revolution seemed to have halted its mad pace. In *Mahogany,* Pil'niak explores the impact of the Bolshevik revolution on ordinary people in a small provincial town. This town, garish and frozen in time, in fact challenges the Bolsheviks' vision of change and rebirth. The iron grip of tradition and the winds of change are the given in Russian social life and literature. Pil'niak brings into this his own sense that change is but illusion.

Like Olesha, Pil'niak detected the ironic perversion of the revolutionary deed. But if Olesha's irony was rooted in the advent of rationality, Pil'niak's irony was hidden in the tenacity of the Russian tradition of venerating the holy fools in Christ's name. In *Mahogany,* Pil'niak gives full and fair play to the tradition of holy fools and the revolutionary heroic deed and self-sacrifice. And, having done so, he penetrates to the pattern of action--a pattern of extolling and deriding, at once hopeful and tragic--which reveals with unusual force his ambiguity towards the contemporary Russian situation. Unlike Gladkov, Kataev, and Makarenko, who, in a Laocoonean twist of the act of faith, extricate themselves from the grip of doubt, Pil'niak's ambiguity and withering faith brought about his arrest, charges of "Trotskyism," and tragic demise in Stalin's concentration camps.

Finally, it was Pil'niak, who saw the contemporary heroic deed as an ironic travesty of the passion of Christ and who actively exploited the metaphor of the "holy fool" to demonstrate the sense of an uninterrupted tradition. These are the aspects of Pil'niak that I shall explore.

Mahogany does not have a plot in the traditional sense, for Pil'niak seems to be more interested in the story of the Russian cultural value of the irrational than in the travails of individual heroes. If I, nonetheless, do extract anything close to the plot, it will come down to the juxtoposition of the two brothers Iakov and Ivan Skudrin. Iakov Skudrin is an ex-serf, a wily wheeler-dealer, a "Russian Voltaire," whose reading of Marx has led him to conclude that the revolution is nothing but fiction. His brother Ivan is a passionate revolutionary, unable to adjust to times of peace and labor. Rejected by his wife and brother Iakov, he lives under the kilns in a forsaken, crumbling brick plant.

Pil'niak finds his "pitch" in the opening tableau of the carnivalesque crowd of "wanderers in Christ's name, prophets, the feeble-minded, holy fools," whom he represents as "synonyms of the twists and turns of the daily life of Mother Russia . . . of a thousand Russian years" (ibid., 375). The anachronistic character of the scene, related in the incantatory notes of a psalm reading, sets the pitch and tone of the narrative. It takes the reader through the millennium to weave its intricate design of the Russian passion for *chudaki* (oddballs). From the scene of prerevolutionary Russia, fixed on venerating the "holy fools in Christ's name," who were "regarded as the adornment of the Church, a brotherhood in Christ, intercessors for the world" (ibid., 377), Pil'niak moves to the scene of the furniture craftsmen, who are fixed on the art of creating furniture masterpieces. However, with the advent of the machine, the art of furniture-making came to naught.

From the preindustrial Russia of the holy fools in Christ's name and the furniture artists, Pil'niak shifts effortlessly to their contemporary heirs, the "holy fools in Communism's name" and the oddballs of the Soviet Russia of the twenties. The new "holy fools" are the ironic relics of Lenin's vision of communist work, and the oddballs are the ironic relics of the mahogany craft--the furniture restorers. Pil'niak's holy fools and oddballs populate two Russias, two polar social realities: the Russia of the East, frozen in tradition, and the Russia of the West, moving toward the future. Each social reality, Pil'niak feels, is animated and energized by its own images and deeds.

Moscow's *Kitai-gorod* (Chinatown), crowded with "the maggots of the holy fools" (ibid., 383), is an ostentatious symbol of the East, the spiritual Russia of "peasants, and town-folks, and noblemen, and merchants" (ibid.). But Pil'niak makes sure that the allusion to the East will not conceal the intensely Russian element of holy foolishness, the Russian veneration of the socially deviant and the psychologically abnormal. Pil'niak felt acutely the Russian suffering and tears of *Kitai-gorod*, the emotions that are almost tangible in the architectural design of Russian churches: "the onion bulbs atop the churches are of course a symbol of the onionish Russian life" (ibid.). The dominant theme of suffering and carnival laughter merges the symbolism of the mundane and the heavenly to efface and revive, to curse and celebrate the unity of the sacred (the church) and the profane (the pungent smell of onion) in the Russian cultural tradition. The onion, the food of the poor and the cause of tears, is transfigured into the symbol of the transcendental, the onion-domes of Russian churches.

But there is also another Russia, the Russia of material culture, which, unlike the culture of spirit, is more prone to change. This is the Russia of the West, host to a different type of oddball: the furniture craftsmen, "the solitary occupants of cellars in towns, and tiny back rooms in the servants' quarters on country estates" (ibid., 385). For Pil'niak, *Mahogany* is the metaphor of passionate, selfless devotion and the intense drive to create. He sees the collapse of craftsmanship and of its creative drive in the advent of industrialization and the beginning of factory production. The creative art is eradicated; instead of it comes the work of restoring and sustaining the masterpieces of the past.

Here the situation inherent in the Russian scene is seized upon and located at the center of Pil'niak's narrative. Pil'niak reveals the power of imagination, both moral and visual, of highest quality. He confronts the contradictory aspects of human deeds within the historical interplay of the spiritual and the material and artfully reveals, cutting across Russian culture, a religious reverence toward human activity that is marginal. This human activity hovers between the deviant and the normal, between the prophet and the holy fool in the inimical society. In the twilight zone between preindustrial and postindustrial Russia there reside other representatives of marginal human activity--the nameless restorers.

Pil'niak fathomed his own tragedy in the craftsmen, whose art degenerates into a sterile act of restoration. His sense of sterile, cheerless work is reflected in the "empty," "vacant" (ibid., 413) eyes of the restorers and in their family name *Bezdetovy* (childless). Pil'niak felt, as Olesha did, that the freedom for creative expression, for individualism, perished in Stalin's Russia as it perished for the craftsman in the age of the machine.

Pil'niak's was the tragedy of the lofty--the passion of Christ--and the base--Ivan the Fool. Here was the passionate truth-seeker, the holy fool, celebrated and belittled by the craftsman turned restorer, the indefatigable survivor. Pil'niak, the holy fool, valiantly spoke the truth; Pil'niak, the craftsman turned restorer, sought to adjust to changed circumstances. The truth-seeker wrote down in his diary at a time of a relative artistic freedom, on September 28, 1923, that truth of expression "is more important than the Communist party and the Russian industrial achievements" (Pil'niak, in Eastman 1934, 105). The craftsman of the Soviet Russia of 1929 no longer had the moral stamina to withstand what Max Eastman, Pil'niak's contemporary, aptly called "crucifixion" (Eastman 1934, 104).

After *Mahogany* was published abroad, Pil'niak, the creative artist "with a genius for disorganized rank, somber realism" was "hounded and baited and branded on the platform in the press from one end of the Soviet Union to the other" and was "deserted by his friends like a leper" (ibid., 109). Pil'niak, the symbol of the deviant in the harsh reality of

Stalin's Russia, took the human form of the tragic solitary figure of the truth seeker.

Mahogany, like all great fiction, is the product of divided sympathies, and we must carefully avoid the temptation to align Pil'niak unequivocally on one side of the conflict. *Mahogany* is a powerful sym- biosis of the despotic tradition of craftsmanship, consummated by a passion for the craft and the poetics of suffering, self-sacrifice, and immortality.

> The art kept going on vodka and cruelty. . . . Sometimes a craftsman would spend decades working on a sofa or dressing table or a small cabinet or a book cabinet. He worked and . . . died, bequething his art to his nephews, for craftsmen were not supposed to have children, and the nephew would either copy his uncle's art or develop it further. A master would die, but the objects would live on. . . . People made love near them and died on the sofas and hid secret correspondence in concealed drawers of escritoires, brides scrutinized their youth, and old women their old age, in the little mirrors of the dressing tables (Pil'niak 1965, 385).

It is possible to observe Pil'niak's fondness for memory, the images of the present sustaining the past. But it is possible to read *Mahogany* as an endorsement of revolutionary change, a plea for rebellion and an attack upon the suffocating conventions of traditional society. This duality of perception, in the form which Pil'niak's ambivalence presented it, inevitably led him to a moment of crucial decision: whether to embrace revolutionary change with all of its gross perversions of Lenin's vision, or, in the spirit of holy fool, to follow blindly the vision and to ignore somber reality, which refuses to yield to the vision. It is the decision about the relationship between the idealized past and the hostile present, between the vision and reality, between morality and survival, and Pil'niak and his hero have to confront it.

It is not by accident that the *okhlomons* seem at closer look to be exact replicas of the mahogany craftsmen, for they are as socially alienated and reclusive as the latter and transcend the wretchedness of their everyday existence by desperately clinging to memory. If the craftsman's passion animates the inanimate mahogany and brings life into the drunken torpor of his existence, the *okhlomon's* passion for the communist ideal animates and brings meaning to a life full of want and deprivation.

In no other novel is the agony of disenchantment so intense and the sense of irony so profound as in the contrasting representations of the two brothers Iakov and Ivan Skudrin. Iakov Karpovich is the crafty wheeler-dealer; his brother Ivan Ozhogov epitomizes the "last true Communist." Ivan's pseudonym, Ozhogov (burning, scalding) alludes to the destructive passion of revolutionary conflagration. It is in Pil'niak's shifting descriptions of the two brothers' worlds that the author's agony and irony reveal themselves.

Iakov's world is permeated by a sense of an ineradicable tradition of masculine despotism and the transcendent vitality of peasant craftiness and wiliness. Iakov is represented as a repulsive eighty-five-year-old with "a slimy little smile, obsequious and spiteful all at once," and "dull-whitish watery eyes" (ibid., 405). He is "a Russian Voltaire" and gives voice to Pil'niak's concerns about the proletarian revolution. His "splutter in his haste to have his say" (ibid., 423) ironically echoes the hopeful language he has picked up from reading Marx in a public library. "Marx's theory of the proletariat," he explains to two traveling craftsmen, "will have to be abandoned soon, because the proletariat itself is bound to disappear" (ibid., 423). Iakov envisions a world "where the only people tending the machines will be engineers, and the proletariat will turn into engineers" (ibid., 423). Therefore, Iakov concludes with a splutter, "the machine requires a knowledgeable man, and instead of a hundred men, as you used to have, all you'll need is one. And that kind of man will be pampered. That's the end of the proletariat!" (ibid., 425)

The ironic context for Iakov's spluttering and its total belittling of the Bolshevik vision reveal Pil'niak in anguish at the futility of the revolution. Pil'niak exemplifies his anguish and abhorrence at the vision gone awry in the circular journey from Iakov Skudrin to the clay pits of a brick factory. This is the world of Ivan Ozhogov and other *okhlomons*, a "stuffy, warm and ascetic burrow" where sleep the men of ideas "that had come to a stop, madmen and drunkards, who had created a strict brotherhood, a strict communism . . . for whom time had stopped in War Communism" (ibid., 431).[4]

Ivan's speech, ignited by a mug of vodka and meager food donated by his brother's wife and other compassionate souls, serves as a somber testament to the irony of the deed. The solemn rhetoric of a eulogy to the Wright brothers, Lenin, and the "last communists in the whole town" is undermined and, finally, mocked and belittled when the speaker confuses myth with reality, the Greek mythical tragedy of Daedalus and Icarus with the successful American airplane tests of the Wright brothers. Ivan's confusion makes poignant the traditional Russian belief that a heroic deed like that of the Wright brothers is inextricably linked to self-sacrifice and glorious death. "For," Ivan intones, "there were once some brothers by the name of Wright. They decided to fly up into the sky and they perished--they fell out of the sky and smashed against the earth. They perished, but men have not abandoned their cause" (ibid., 433).

Ivan's celebration of Lenin, the Wright brothers, and the ideas of the last communists is toned down by another round of vodka. Pil'niak's convictions, which oscillate feverishly between the lofty and the base, become even more shaky in Ivan's attempts to keep the ideal untarnished by the violence and blood that have sustained it. Here is the scene:

> Ognev interrupted Ozhogov: "What deeds we did! How we fought!
> . . . Ognev was interrupted by Pozharov, who asked: "How do you
> hold your saber? How do you hold your thumb when you make a
> slash, bent or straight?" . . .
> "Comrades," Ozhogov spoke up softly, and his face twisted in *mad*
> [emphasis added] pain, "today we should be talking about ideas, about
> great ideas, and not about swinging sabers!" (ibid., 435)

The crude "fall" from the heights of communist rhetoric to the pits of actual brutality of the heroic deed, from "the great ideas" to "the swinging sabers," reveals Pil'niak's despair at the chasm between the ideal and the real. It is the despair of a believer in the absolute, for whom lack of wholesomeness spells madness.

In citing the above scene, I have intentionally emphasized the word "mad," for throughout the novel Pil'niak frequently associates Ozhogov's state of mind with madness and insanity. This explicit reference to psychological deviance takes us back to Pil'niak's central metaphor of the holy fool.

The narrative, which opens with the nauseating details of the veneration of holy fools in the Russian tradition, explodes in an ironic revelation: the "last Communist," Ivan Ozhogov, has become the town's holy fool. Pil'niak introduces the transfigured image of Ivan Ozhogov, the holy fool of Communist deed, with an exact replica of the opening metaphor: "the holy fools of Holy Mother Russia in Christ's name. These twists represented the beauty of daily life" (ibid., 478). Ivan, Pil'niak maliciously suggests, is "a vagabond mendicant, the holy fool Lazarus--a holy fool of Soviet Russia in the name of justice, an intercessor for the world and for communism" (ibid., 481). The irony is here, and it is complete. In no other piece of Soviet literature has the image of the deed been so tarnished and degraded by an implicit reference to the native celebration of holy foolishness.

Here is Pil'niak celebrating Ivan, the heroic fighter for the idea. "The town revered Ivan, as the Russians over the centuries have been wont to revere holy fools, whose lips spoke the truth, and who are ready to die to uphold the truth" (ibid., 480). Pil'niak strips the veneer of holiness and heroism to expose sobering facts--"each and every one of them had his own crazy pet project: one of them had a fixation on correspondence with the proletariat from Mars, another proposed to catch all adult fish in Volga and use the money to pay the cost of building iron bridges across the Volga" (ibid., 480). It is a celebration that merges heroic deed and madness, that merges the sublime--the homage and veneration accorded to the heroic deed in the name of social justice--and the base-- mental derangement.

If Pil'niak has established continuity between the Communists and their historic progenitors, the holy fools, if their heroic deeds are tainted by mental disease and social deviance, it was because Pil'niak looked around and, like Chekhov before him, saw no escape for the human creative spirit and no venue for human passion and deed. This is one of the major "epiphanies" in the novel, one of the major moments of recognition that the present is mocking the travesty of the passion of Christ and that the heroic deed of suffering and self-sacrifice is as devoid of meaning as the "empty" eyes of the restorers.

It might be that Pil'niak deprives the deed of honor and meaning because he feels that contemporary society and the social order it has created are deprived of them too. It is a cheerless, moss-covered, grim society of despotic and wily household masters, a crafty and inept band of the "town bosses," who juggle, reshuffle, and "bungle with passion the prerevolutionary wealth" (ibid., 396). It is also the social order that celebrates the poverty of the "loafers, blabbermouths, philosophers, sluggards and oafs" (ibid., 497) which demolishes the wealth of the hard- working, the efficient, the prudent, and the rational.

The irony is here, and it is pervasive and insidious. Human passion and the deed of suffering and self-sacrifice reek of physical and moral stagnation.

Conclusion

The historical development of the Russian perception of work between the 1890s and the 1930s was a complex process of negotiation between the Russian and his contemporary social institutions and practices. This process of negotiation was molded and defined by the Russian's continuous fascination with the suffering and the martyrdom of Jesus Christ. The persisting moods and motivations evoked by the image of the passion of Christ showed signs of remarkable resilience and vitality among all the authors reviewed in this study. Their hallmark was the celebration of readiness for suffering and self-sacrifice, which suggested a kind of ascetic labor divorced from the mundane work, emancipated from history, and bereft of any familial and social attachments. This Russian perception of purposeful human activity bore the stigma of a protracted history of tyranny and servitude, and of rupture between the past and the present, as well as the hallmark of continuity, of successful adaptations and adjustments--engrams of the image of the passion of Christ in the cultural memory.

The guiding fiction of this kind of perception, and one of its key tenets, was that purposeful human activity, work, should pave the road to universal salvation. Herein lies the key difference between the Russian and the Puritan perceptions of work. Whereas Russian Orthodoxy celebrated the eternal life of heaven and declared earthly existence transitory and meaningless, the Puritan work ethic emphasized mundane economic activities as moral duty to God and, therefore, unlike the Russian, sought personal salvation. Thus the Puritan or Western meaning of labor, although mindful of the physical pain associated with it, nonetheless celebrated the process of reproduction and renewal. Its

Russian counterpart, on the other hand, was devoid of Western dialectical meaning and its implied reward or, in this sense, hope. While the Puritan's concern with economic activity--profits and money-making --was rooted in the value of rationality, in the belief in the power of human reason to solve every issue, Russian Orthodoxy censored profits and money-making activities. What was left then of the Russian Orthodox belief about mundane economic activity was the tendency to view labor as the source of pain and to emphasize the value of suffering and self-sacrifice. The Russian Orthodoxy's preoccupation with suffering, self-sacrifice, and universal salvation underscored the value of the irrational and the distrust of human reason. Consequently, when the Russian revolted, like the Russian schismatics and Lev Tolstoy did, against the concept of universal salvation, their shift from universal to personal salvation represented the adjustment and adaptation of the Western concept within the context of the traditional Russian value of suffering and self-sacrifice.

With the increasing pace of Russia's industrialization drive at the beginning of the century and the intensifying politico-economic struggle against the tsarist regime,. the Russian Christian symbol of the passion of Christ gave rhythm and shape to the Russian meaning of purposeful human activity. The Russian articulated his perception of work within the context of Russian industrialization, which was marked by persisting despotic police rule, a heavy tax burden upon the peasantry, and limited access for the intelligentsia to the existing power structure. The Russian's interpretation of the double message of the conflict between him and the coercive authority, of defeat or victory, yields illuminating insights into the peasant's and intellectual's conceptions of response to coercion, negotiated by the Russian Orthodox image of the passion of Christ.

Given the intensity of the tensions, human work was seen as either a challenge to contemporary practices and institutions or as a surrender to outside pressure. For those who, like the Russian peasant, felt the futility of either of those ends, manipulation, trickery, and deceit became the core values in the meaning of purposeful human activity and the fulcrum for fending off outside pressure. Work as a challenge to contemporary practices was expounded upon in the revolutionary maxims of struggle against the existing political and socioeconomic reality. A challenge to contemporary practices was the call for hope, the promise of salvation through self-sacrifice. Work as surrender to suffering was propounded in Tolstoy's maxim of nonresistance to oppression and in his call for self-sacrifice in order to exercise the inner freedom of will in cultivating self-perfection and in accepting moral responsibility. Work as manipulation, trickery, and deceit was expressed in the peasant's formula of survival in a hostile environment, which violated his sense of justice. Within this context of survival, suffering and self-sacrifice was seen as devoid of glory and honor, and the meaning of labor was shorn of the sense of hope. With the perception of labor divested of hope and suffering and self-sacrifice deglamorized and without honor, manipulation, trickery, and deceit are recognized as valuable for leverage in dealing with an otherwise destructive experience.

There were several strands of collusion and negotiation that were explored in this study, strands which I see as being of paramount importance in the Russian historical meaning of work. They include the Tolstoyan, the Christian intelligentsia's, and the Bolsheviks' maxims of work, as well as the peasant's, the revolutionary's, and the Russian intellectual's perceptions of work.

The Tolstoyan and the Christian intelligentsia's maxim of work was both an engram and a message. It was an engram of the passion of Christ; and it was a message which strove to produce an ideological impact of its own on the public at large. Tolstoy believed that altruistic work, unburdened by the pursuit of ambition and pleasure, was the only path to salvation. He felt that purposeful human activity had to emulate Christ's moral choice of self-renunciation and self-sacrifice. This belief was echoed in Bulgakov's moral-religious credo of the monastic ethic of work, which sought to energize mundane everyday human activity with Russian spirituality. It is a sign of the depth and tenacity of the image of the passion of Christ that Lenin's vision of the communist ethic of work echoed Tolstoy's maxims. Furthermore, Tolstoy's moral-philosophical teaching about the virtues of altruistic physical work as a means of liberating a person from the pangs of temptations and unsatisfied desires and giving him real happiness became the driving force and spirit behind Makarenko's school of thought about socialization in the ethic of work. It was in the nature of Tolstoy's moral rectitude that he was among the first Russian intellectuals to enunciate the revolutionary shift from Christ the sufferer to Christ the activist, whose self-sacrifice was a bold act that asserted that individual free will is of paramount importance in the fate of mankind.

Tolstoy and Berdyayev gave voice to the deep Russian deep yearning for free will, which was challenged and diminished by the despotic social reality. Their call for moral free will lent force and fervor to the Russian argument against the institutional authority of the State and the Church. The radicalism of the Russian political structure was negotiated by the radicalism of its ideological opposition. Tolstoy's and Berdyayev's visions, in their search for the absolute truth, were untarnished by doubts and unmarred by vacillations.

The voice of experience sounded in the literary narratives and folktales, although distinctly hostile to authority and its institutions, nonetheless negotiated a somewhat fuzzier image of work. Let us first take a look at the Russian peasant, whose perceptions were the refractions of the image of the passion of Christ negotiated by his intimate experience of pain and physical suffering. Labor was, therefore, perceived as an inevitable evil, which sustained life, but did not carry hope of happiness. I explored the interplay of the image and social reality in the semantic paradigm of the Russian concept of "suffering"-- the conflation of the spiritual and the mundane, of the ecclesiastical image and summer fieldwork. The semantic paradigms of the Russian *krestianin* (peasant) and *strada* (summer fieldwork) reveal a conscious convergence between the peasant's image of physical suffering as the result of hard work and the spiritual image of physical and mental suffering before the crucifixion. The Russian peasant defined *strada* in terms of suffering and the process of dying. The root of the Russian word *krestianin--krest* (the cross)--invokes Christ carrying the cross to Golgotha and the peasant's sense of partaking alongside Jesus Christ in the same torment of suffering. This collusion of the spiritual and the mundane conveyed the mood of the Russian peasant, who grappled to perceive the eschatological message of hope in mundane suffering and pain.

The teasing out of the structures of signification in Russian folktales revealed a dent in the promise of salvation: the peasant's mocking belit-tling of the act of crucifixion as devoid of reason. With the sense of hope in the heavenly kingdom erased, the peasant recognized that his work meant survival rather than redemption. Manipulation, trickery, and conniving took the central position in the peasant's paradigm of the meaning of work, for they were his unique ways of imparting meaning to what he perceived as inherently hopeless social reality. Given the agricultural nature of Russian society at the turn of the century, it would be logical to conclude that peasant perceptions of work played a crucial role in the historical development of the Russian meaning of work.

Unlike the peasant, the Russian intellectual tended to look for the moral, rather than the pragmatic, meanings of human work. The central strain in the Russian intellectual's perception of work was defined by a desire, akin to that of the peasant, to make sense of human work in a hostile environment within the paradigm of the meaning evoked by the image of the passion of Christ. Bunin and Chekhov, for example, nursed strong doubts about the salubrious effects of suffering and renunciation of the mundane, which were extolled by Tolstoy. Chekhov denounced Russian preoccupation with suffering as a human weakness which was averse to exerting itself, to putting up resistance to outside pressure. He condemned the Russian celebration of suffering as a deadly malaise of the Russian intelligentsia. Bunin, too, challenged the benefits of suffering and revealed its paralyzing effect on the human psyche and on work. Bunin and Chekhov were convinced that the scourge of suffering inflicted on man in his everyday existence deprived him of the will to act; suffering, they held, was associated with an overwhelming feeling of apathy and was nurtured by a sense of fatalism and resignation. Work, consequently, was recognized as an inevitable bondage and a curse.

Bunin and Chekhov castigated the educated and intellectually ambitious Russian for being short on action. However, their own prejudice against the ambition of the activist and the doer, in a peculiar Russian twist, resonated with the familiar note of the Tolstoyan foreboding against work driven by ambition, lest it bring misery and unhappiness. Whereas Tolstoy preached self-abnegation and self-sacrifice as a way out, Bunin and Chekhov felt ambivalent about any escape from the odium of being.

If Tolstoy celebrated suffering and Bunin and Chekhov condemned it as a curse, Vrubel saw it as a representation of the duality of human experience--the tragedy of dissent and the harsh celebration of defiance. Rebellion against authority, while doomed to defeat and fraught with the pain of physical suffering, was perceived by him as endowed with a sense of spiritual glory and victory. It was the same mood of rebellion that animated a small, but, nonetheless, vocal group of Russian social democrats who called for the complete destruction of existing institutions and social practices. All human activity that, however slightly, sought to circumvent direct confrontation, to cushion the clash, or to modify the existing structure was vehemently condemned as reactionary. All labor was denounced as inherently exploitative.

Andreev and Gorky shifted the emphasis in the image of the passion of Christ from Christ the sufferer to Christ the activist. This was a passionate image of Savior whose self-sacrifice ushered in the liberation of mankind and the birth of New Man. Although Andreev's belief in self-sacrifice tended to vacillate between his allegiance to scientific endeavor and to the revolutionary deed, Gorky threw his whole weight of oratory and persuasion to the defense of the revolutionary heroic deed. Both of them, however, seemed quite firm in their conviction that man was only an appendage to the lofty task of universal salvation. Andreev and Gorky invested their secularized martyrs, in the name of science and the revolution, with the passionate zeal of Christian believers. Like Tolstoy, Bulgakov, and Berdyayev, Andreev and Gorky moved toward moral insight of human endeavor. All of them celebrated the passion of Christ, but Tolstoy, Bulgakov, and Berdyayev pinned their hopes of redemption on the introverted parochialism of the past, whereas Andreev and Gorky envisioned hope in the extroverted internationalism of the future.

That was a cardinal divergence between the Christian and the revolutionary intelligentsia, for whom suffering was both the punishment and the victory, and the Russian peasant, who seemed ambivalent about his ability to gain glory and victory by means other than manipulation, trickery, and deceit. Consequently, the prerevolutionary Russian meaning of work effectively foreclosed the possibility of embracing utilitarian and pragmatic notions of work animated by individual aspirations and ambitions. The continuous emphasis on eschatological salvation exposed a deeply rooted scorn for individual ambition and material well-being. The intellectuals' love of the extreme incapacitated them and made them short on action.

The Marxist revolutionary idea, a hostage of the native image, was grafted on intrinsically alien soil, which was devoid of the Western tradition of democracy and rationalism. For all its criticism of the capitalist system of production, appropriation, and distribution, the Marxist revolutionary idea was the product of Western pressures. The Western ideas of work--Marxist, socialist, and non-socialist alike--betray a common framework of cultural assumptions: the Western liberal, optimistic belief in the power of human reason; belief in the power of hope in the inevitability of progress, and glorification of productive work as the source of social life. Unlike the optimistic Westerner, the Russian tended to view the concept of progress with deep suspicion and doubt. The Russian questioned the inhumanity of dispassionate reason, glorified the pain of suffering, and celebrated the heroic deed of self-sacrifice. Lenin and other Bolshevik leaders adapted Marxism within the Russian context of self-sacrifice and universal salvation. Marx's celebration of the creative powers of capitalist labor, which was alien to the Russian cultural paradigm of work values, remained muted.

The Russian revolutionary saluted the redeemed man, the militant interventionist, the savior of mankind, and, paradoxically, immediately deprived him of independence under the rule of party discipline. The paradox did not stop there. The revolutionary work ethic celebrated the redemptive powers of work and concurrently denounced them as degrading and exploitative. It insisted on rational thinking and immediately denounced it as detached and inhuman. The seeds of the incompatibility between Russian convictions and an adopted Western ideology of the work ethic were already imbedded in the early stages of the Russian revolutionary quest for change.

After the Bolshevik revolution, the process of negotiation between the Russian and his social reality, curiously, had changed little from the prerevolutionary tradition of challenge and surrender to outside pressure. The Russian love of the extreme, ardent belief in human perfectibility, and intense absorption with eschatological visions and self-sacrifice manifested themselves in the Bolsheviks' visions of the communist work ethic. Ethnic pressures notwithstanding, the Bolsheviks' vision of work represented their growing realization that a viable work ethic could be achieved only by wedding Western efficiency and mercantile rationality to the Russian image of self-sacrifice and the heroic deed. The leadership's attempts to celebrate the mutually exclusive notions of the self-effacing revolutionary deed and efficiency, of self-sacrifice and mercantile rationality, revealed with unusual power and clarity the Russian's ambivalence toward Western values of work. What made the Bolsheviks' ambivalence particularly poignant was the fact that despite their disturbing awareness of the debilitating effects of the native image, they themselves remained deeply entangled in the cultural web of signification created by this image.

The Bolsheviks' vision of communist work reverberated in the emergent drama of Soviet industrialization depicted in the narratives of the believers in the Socialist salvation--Gladkov, Kataev, and Makarenko. It was in the nature of Russian cultural values that both Gladkov and Kataev, despite their ardent belief in socialist redemption, experienced pangs of doubt about the moral underpinnings of man's celebration of the machine and his violation of nature. However, they seemed to suppress their doubts and recover their shaken convictions in an incredulous leap of faith to the redemptive powers of socialism. Their heroes, like the proverbial converts to Christianity, were counterpoised to the existing social behavior and practices. They stood above the crowd and were ferociously independent; they were driven by social ideals and undefiled by personal ambition. Their perceptions of work were strongly colored by a powerful mix of Christian zeal and Western self-reliance.

All the authors reviewed in this study exhibited a strong sense of human work as a matter of passion. Their militant assault on traditional practices and beliefs was, however, fraught with irony, for "traditional" meant "rational" and "bureaucratic." It evoked hostile visions of the corrupt and treacherous tsarist bureaucracy. The meaning of work flowing from this perception reenacted the old Russian prejudices. For Gladkov, it was a matter of divided perceptions and the growing realization that work in this socialist reality was partially a matter of survival and required masculinity, conniving, and wit, which were at the core of the Russian peasant's ethic of work. If at the end of *Cement* Gladkov rediscovered faith in the saving power of the passion of Christ, it might have been because he, like Kataev and Makarenko, tried to overcome his tortuous doubts in a powerful leap of faith.

In Kataev's *Time, Forward!*, work became an affirmation of the belief that the New Communist Man became a god who was changing his social and natural environment. Kataev defined the ethic of work within the paradigm of meanings associated with a vigorous assault on the external restrictions: time and the inherent frailty of the human body. Despite his strenuous attempts to celebrate the Bolsheviks' ideas of rationality and efficiency, Kataev seemed unable to extricate himself from the Russian value of self-sacrifice and the heroic deed. But it was Makarenko who elevated the myth of the heroic deed of challenge, defiance, and self-sacrifice to the pedagogical maxims of socialization in the communist ethic of work.

Makarenko was firmly convinced that for educational work to achieve its desired ends it had to be driven by passion rather than by the detached rationality of pedagogical science. It was his root principle, his position, and his doctrine that work is a deed exercised in the center of the life of a group, a matter of *podvizhnechestvo* (heroic selfless devotion). In coming to his position, Makarenko drew on the Bolsheviks' vision of communist work, but he also lent a peculiar Russian folk flavor to the process of socialization--love for religious ritual curiously blended with military discipline. Makarenko's distrust, which was akin to that of the Russian peasant, of the positive effects of physical work, other than that which was life-sustaining, revealed itself in his insistence that socialization in the work ethic should be intrinsically linked to teaching endurance of suffering. Makarenko strove to educate his readers in the religion of work by means that were familiar to the Russian religious believer--the adulation of suffering and self-sacrifice. For Makarenko, the personal self-sacrifice of turning hardened criminals into skilled, socially useful professionals suggested the ultimate work ethic, the heroic deed.

Gladkov's, Kataev's, and Makarenko's celebration of the militant masculinity of the collective-oriented heroic deed seemed to Olesha and Pil'niak like a mocking violation of what the native image held dear: freedom of will and the value of the irrational. This was the context for their perceptions of purposeful human activity. In this new age of industrialization, Olesha saw, as Tolstoy did, in the advent of the machine age the loss of humanism, the sacrifice of man to the Moloch of industrial production. And like Gladkov, Olesha had deep misgivings about the collective's claims on the individual's allegiance, which he thought rendered human feelings sterile and extinct. He experienced the most strenuous doubts about the value of the newly emergent work ethic of industrial society with its emphasis on rationality and collectivism.

Consistent with the traditional Russian attitude, Olesha suspected that the heroic deed consisted of two polar absolutes: self-sacrifice and glorious death, or complete resignation and the apathy of surrender.

If Olesha was ambivalent about collectivism and rationality in the communist ethic of work, Pil'niak had no doubt that change in the small provincial town was but an illusion. Pil'niak detected the ironic perversion of the revolutionary deed by the tenacity of Russian tradition. It was Pil'niak who saw the contemporary heroic deed as an ironic travesty of the passion of Christ. Pil'niak explored the Russian perception of the heroic deed in both the material and the spiritual cultures of Stalin's Russia. He felt, as Olesha did, that freedom of will and the freedom for creative expression, for individualism, perished in Stalin's Russia, as it had perished for the craftsman in the age of the machine. Pil'niak the passionate truth seeker, negotiated his survival with his double, Pil'niak the survivor, who sought to manipulate his environment, to adjust to changed circumstances. Pil'niak the prophet established continuity between the Communists, the believers in Lenin's vision of the communist ethic of work, and their historic progenitors, the holy fools, whose heroic deeds were tainted by mental disease and social deviance. But Pil'niak the realist saw no escape and no venue for human passion and deed. For him, who saw no light at the end of the tunnel, work became the art of survival--manipulation, trickery, or death. Thus, work--purposeful human activity--was not seen by the Russian, as it was by the Westerner, as a means for personal gratification and self-fulfillment.

The impediments of the native image are only too obvious. The individual never had a chance to recognize the idea that work might be a process of personal salvation. The Russian negotiated his release from the hostile environment by age-old-means--manipulation and conniving. The Western notion of work ethic acquired a different set of meanings in Stalin's Russia. Therefore, despite fundamental changes in the political and socioeconomic structure of Russian society, the Russian perception of work exhibited remarkable persistence and endurance between 1890 and 1935.

The conclusion flowing from the this study challenges the ideological assumptions and theoretical presumptions of developmental theories. The findings of this research reveal a basic flaw in current developmental discourse, in modernization, dependency, and world-system theories--the neglect of the human agent and his perception of contemporary socioeconomic and political reality.

The persistence and resilience of the traditional Russian perceptions of work suggest several fallacies in modernization theory. First, the dichotomy between the traditional and the modern proves to be unfeasible. Second, the optimistic belief in the power of ideology to socialize people in "modern" values fails to materialize. Third, the assumption that modernizing societies exhibit the same pattern of development neglects the cultural peculiarities of Russian modernization, which industrialized without the democratic changes that accompanied the process of modernization in the West.

This study of the Russian perceptions of work also demonstrates that the dependency school's assumption that the capitalist system is the dominant variable in cultural institutions and relations is untenable. The dependency theory, which reduces a complex process of social change to a single denominator--economic dependency--fails to account for the absence of "automatic change" in the Russian perception of work in the course of modernization. The findings of this study show that economic change in the course of modernization is negotiated and accommodated within the cultural system of beliefs.

The world-system approach, which takes research away from the realm of the particular into the realm of the global, fails to explain the particularities of the Russian course of modernization and industrialization, which, as the findings of this study reveal, were defined and shaped by cultural particularism.

The findings of this study, which point to persistent discontinuities between the Russian's perception of work and his social structure, support the Geertzian model of social change, whereby cultural and social aspects of life are introduced as independent variables and yet are mutually dependent factors. Within this conceptual framework, what occurred between 1890 and 1935 was not so much the destruction of the traditional Russian way of life as the construction of a new one, the search for a more generalized, more flexible pattern of beliefs. It is within this complex conception of the relations between religious belief and secular social life that we can account for the process of transformation from the image of the suffering Christ to the image of the suffering peasant, from Christian martyr to communist martyr.

The religious image of the passion of Christ and its underlying conceptions of suffering, self-sacrifice, and salvation have constituted the paradigm of the Russian meaning of work. It was the image that shaped and molded the Russian Marxist's sociopolitical thought. The configuration of such dissimilar meanings of work in the Bolsheviks' vision of communist work as Russian self-sacrifice and salvation and Western rationality and efficiency displays the complex semantic structure of the ideological symbol conferred by the interplay between the semantic structure and the social reality of modernizing Russia. The key to the persistence and resilience of the traditional Russian conception of work is offered in Geertz's conceptualization of the tensions between local, traditional and general, historical movement. Looked upon within this framework of tensions, the Bolsheviks' vision of communist work represented an attempt to cast a historical movement--the modernization drive--into a specific symbol that would combine Russian and Western conceptions of work and perpetuate the process of what Geertz called "collective self-redefinition." Although the Russian meaning of work in Stalin's Russia was tragic, it carried the seeds of hope.

For the first time in Russian history, the Russian is now being given a taste and firsthand experience of democratic rule and political freedom. Given the Russian's deep-seated distrust of authority and social and legal practices, it would take an educational effort of immense proportions to socialize the young in respect to the rule of democratic law and order. It is a formidable challenge to Russian pedagogical science to look for effective ways to channel the Russian yearning for freedom of will into creative work that will see the promise of hope in the emerging demo-cratic social order. The resurgence of the Russian religious spirit could strive to fulfill Bulgakov's call for endowing all aspects of social work with spiritual fervor, will, and perseverance. In such efforts however difficult, however beset with doubts and uncertainties, there lies the prospect for a viable ethic of work, for increased chances of survival for the embryonic Russian democracy.

Notes

INTRODUCTION

1. I believe that female and male perceptions of work differ. Therefore, female ethnic Russian perceptions of work would warrant separate research.

2. This image, I suspect, is of a more venerable age.

3. For a more detailed description of Russian religious values see George Fedotov, *The Russian Religious Mind* (Cambridge: Harvard University Press, 1946); and Nikolai Berdyayev, "Russkaia Religioznaia Ideia," in *Problemy Russkogo Religioznogo Soznaniia,* (Berlin: YMCA Press, 1923).

4. See Hanna Arendt, *The Human Condition* (Garden City, NY: Doubleday Anchor Books, 1959), p. 314.

5. To name only a few: The failed military coup by the Decembrists (1825), who were trying to liberalize the Russian regime; the revolution of 1905; and the bourgeois revolution of 1917.

6. For instance, the abolition of serfdom (1861) failed to bring democratic change to Russia; and Russian institutions of democratic representation--*Zemstvos* (Local Councils) and *Duma* (Representative Assembly)--either had very limited political power or were abolished or dismissed if they were seen as a serious challenge to the government.

7. The Russian schism started at the turn of the seventeenth century. However, it was successfully contained by the state and the official Russian Orthodox church. For details see N. M. Nikol'skii, *Istoriia Russkoi Tserkvi* (Moscow: Izd-vo Politicheskoi Literatury, 1988).

8. Smelser obviously refers to Khrushchev's tinkering with the idea of decentralization. The idea suffered a resounding crash and ejected him, disgraced, from his position of power.

9. For more information see Andre Gunder Frank, *Capitalism and Underdevelopment in Latin America: Historical Studies of Chile and Brazil* (New York: Monthly Review Press, 1969); and Samir Amin, *Unequal Development: An Essay on the Social Formation of Peripheral Capitalism* (New York: Monthly Review Press, 1976).

10. For example, Alexander Gershenkron writes, "The great spurt of the 1890s had prepared for the subsequent continuation of [industrial] growth." In "Patterns of Economic Development," in *The Transformation of Russian Society,* ed. Cyril E. Black (Cambridge: Harvard University Press, 1960), p. 56.

Chapter 1
THE CASE AGAINST THE PRESENT

1. See Edward Crankshaw, *The Shadows of the Winter Palace* (New York: Viking, 1976).

2. See Boris Kagarlitsky, *The Thinking Reed*, trans. Brian Pearce (London and New York: Verso, 1988).

3. Quoted in A. S. Prugavin, *Raskol i Sektantstvo v Russkoi Narod-noi Zhizni* (Moscow: n.p., 1905), pp. 25-26.

Chapter 3
THE FUNCTION OF RELIGION: TOLSTOY, BULGAKOV, BERDYAYEV

1. See V. V. Zenkovsky, *A History of Russian Philosophy*, vol. 2, trans. George L. Kline (New York: Columbia University Press, 1953), p. 754.

2. Nikolai Berdyayev, "Smysl Tvorchestva" (1916), quoted in V. V. Zenkovsky, *Russkie Mysliteli i Evropa* (Paris: YMCA Press, n.d.), pp. 275-76.

3. Ibid. p. 276.

4. A political movement among the Russian intelligentsia in the 1870s.

5. See L. N. Tolstoy, "Ne Delanie" in *Sochineniia Grafa L. N. Tolstogo (Collected Works of Count L. N. Tolstoy)*, part 14, 10th ed. (Moscow: Tovarishch. I. N. Kushnerev i Ko, 1897).

6. Citing the report of 1890-1891 of the Holy Synod's chief prosecutor, Prugavin confirmed that *mostly educated* (emphasis added) people supported Tolstoy's belief that Jesus Christ's death should be considered

salvation only if it served as an inspiring example for all sufferers. Quoted in A. S. Prugavin, *O L've Tolstom i Tolstovtsakh (Concerning Leo Tolstoy and His Disciples)* (Moscow: n.p., 1911), p. 186.

7. I owe the background information on Bulgakov to V. V. Zenkovsky. See V. V. Zenkovsky. *A History of Russian Philosophy,* vol. 2, pp. 890-91.

8. St. Sergei (1314?-92), who was canonized in 1452, was one of the outstanding Russian churchmen of the fourteenth century and one of the most revered figures in Russian religious history. See *Signposts*, M. S. Schatz and J. E. Zimmerman, eds. and trans., (Irvine, CA: Charles Schlacks, Jr., 1986), p. 167.

9. Stepan Razin (1671) and Emel'ian Pugachev (1742-1775) were the leaders of the bloody peasant revolts. See *Signposts*, pp. 165-66.

10. Berdyaev, "Specters of the Russian Revolution," *Out of the Depths*, trans. and ed. William F. Woehrlin (Irvine, CA: Charles Schlacks, Jr., 1986), pp. 41-42.

11. Berdyaev, "Philosophical Verity and Intelligentsia Truth," *Signposts*, p. 15.

Chapter 4
THE CURSE OF LIVING: BUNIN AND CHEKHOV

1. Anton Chekhov, "Palata No 6" in *Rasskazy* (St. Petersburg: A. F. Marks, 1900), pp. 131-196.

2. I. A. Bunin, "Derevnia" in *Sobranie Sochinenii*, vol. II (Berlin: Petropolis, 1934), pp. 7-192.

3. Breed of a Russian hunting dog.

4. The great Russian poet of the nineteenth century who was killed in a duel.

5. An eminent poet and prose-writer, who was a contemporary of Pushkin and was also killed in a duel.

6. A nineteenth century Russian philosopher and publicist.

7. A nineteenth century poet who was executed for participating in the Decembrists' insurrection of 1925.

8. Serge Kryzytsky, Bunin's biographer, cites Bunin's short-lived venture into coopering and making hoops. See Serge Kryzytsky, *The Works of Ivan Bunin* (The Hague: Mouton, 1971), p. 21.

Chapter 5
APOTHEOSIS OF HEROIC DEED: ANDREEV AND GORKY

1. Russian religious movement close to Protestantism in its teaching.

The advocacy of violence Bonch-Bruevich cites further on was voiced, according to his own study, only by a small part of the schismatics. Notably, in 1922, after the revolutionary fervor had subsided, Bonch-Bruevich wrote admiringly about their ethic of work. For a more detailed analysis of the Russian schism see V. D. Bonch-Bruevich, *Iz Mira Sektantov* (n.p., 1922).

2. This desire for reform and the belief in self-sacrifice among the Russian schismatics was also noted by Prugavin, another eminent student of the Russian schism. See A. S. Prugavin, *Raskol Vverkhu* (St. Peterburg: n.p., 1909).

3. Maxim Gorky, "Mat'(Mother)" in *Sobranie Sochinenii* vol. 4 (Moscow: Gos. Izd-vo Khud. Lit-ra, 1960).

4. It is possible to speculate that Gorky drew an analogy between Pavel and St. Paul, Christ's apostle, whose revelation in the desert turned him into Christ's staunch supporter.

5. According to Irwin Weil, Gorky became involved in the revolutionary activities in the late 1880s. See I. Weil, *Gorky* (New York: Random House, 1966), p. 45.

6. See Weil, *Gorky,* p. 15.

7. In *"Chto Delat'?"* (1902), Lenin enunciated his views on the party as an organization of professional revolutionaries tightly controlled by a single chain of command. See V. I. Lenin, "Chto Delat'?" in vol. 1 of *Sobranie Sochinenii*, 5th ed. (Moscow: Izd-vo Polit. Lit-ry, 1960), pp. 1-192.

8. *Kenotic (adj.)*, *kenosis (n)* means the relinquishment of the form of God by Christ in becoming man and suffering death.

Chapter 6
THE BOLSHEVIKS' VISIONS OF COMMUNIST WORK

1. Lenin, "The New Economic Policy and the Tasks of the Political Education Department," in *Selected Works* IX (New York: International Publishers, 1937), p. 267.

2. Lenin quoted in Philip G. Roeder, *Soviet Political Dynamics* (New York: Harper and Row, 1988), p. 5.

3. Decree of June 15, 1918 "Nationalization of the Largest Enterprises," quoted in Zigurds L. Zile, ed., *Ideas and Forces in Soviet Legal History* (New York: Oxford University Press, 1992), pp. 127-28.

4. Decree of February 26, 1919 "On the Functioning of the Supreme National Economic Council," quoted in Zile, *Ideas,* pp. 129-30.

5. "Constitution of the RSFSR of 1918." (RSFSR stands for Russian

Soviet Federal Socialist Republic.) In Zile, *Ideas*, p. 66.

6. *War Communism* was a program enacted by the Bolsheviks between 1918 to 1920. Aimed at building a communist society, this program led to almost total control by the Bolsheviks over the economy. The peasants and artisans, as well as factories, had no right to sell their products but were obligated to turn them over to the state. The state, in its turn, supplied them with what they needed. Money was abolished, and individual private enterprises were regarded as doomed to extinction. Peasants, artisans and workers alike received food rations.

7. Lenin in "Verbatim Record of the Fourteenth Sessions of the Tenth Congress of the Russian Communist Party (Bolsheviks) March 15, 1921." Cited in Zile, *Ideas*, p. 147.

8. An article from Pravda, May 17, 1919, "Working in a Revolutionary Way (A Communist Sabbath)," cited by Lenin on June 28, 1919, in "A Great Beginning," in Lenin, *Selected Works* IX (New York: International Publishers, 1937), p. 424.

9. Lenin, "From the Destruction of the Ancient Social System to the Creation of the New," in Lenin, *Selected Works,* p. 447.

10. In what Lenin called a "strategic retreat," the New Economic Policy of state controlled capitalism was announced. See V. Lenin, *The New Economic Policy and the Tasks of the Political Education Department* (New York: International Publishers, 1937), p. 259.

11. See Lenin's letters sent between November 1920 and March 1923, in Vladimir Lenin, *Collected Works,* 45 (London: Lawrence & Wishart, 1970).

12. A prominent Marxist who had moved away from Marxism to Christianity and participated in the forums of *Signposts* and *Out of the Depths.*

13. Lenin, "On Cooperation" in *Selected Works* IX (New York: International Publishers, 1937), p. 405.

14. Lenin, "Six Thesis Concerning the Immediate Tasks of Soviet Power" (1918). In Zile *Ideas,* p. 127.

15. Compare with the Marxist argument that socialism is superior to capitalism.

16. In his speech on the Right Deviation in the Communist Party of the Soviet Union (bolsheviks) (CPSU) (b) in April 1929, Stalin accused Bukharin of betraying Marxism. Bukharin, according to Stalin, wrongly assumed that "the class struggle must subside and pass away so that the abolition of classes may be brought about." See Zile *Ideas,* p. 200. Bukharin was executed in 1938.

17. See Lenin's quote on p. 90.

Chapter 7
THE NEW CHRISTIANS IN THE SOVIET INDUSTRIALIZATION: GLADKOV, KATAEV, MAKARENKO

1. Gladkov's biographical data has been taken from L. N. Ul'rikh, *Letopis' Zhizni i Tvorchestva Gladkova* (Tashkent: Fan, 1982).

2. A city at the Black Sea.

3. Cheka was the antecedent of the KGB. From Kataev's autobiographic note quoted in Robert Russel, *Valentin Kataev* (Boston: Twayne Publishers, 1981), p. 16.

4. Stalin called the period between 1928-1939 "The Revolution from Above." Stalin quoted in Roeder, *Soviet Political Dynamics*, p.74.

5. See Stalin's speech, XIV s'iezd VKP (1931) cited in A. Kemp-Welch, *Stalin and the Literary Intelligentsia, 1928-1938* (New York: St. Martin's Press, 1991), p. 90.

6. A Soviet literary historian and critic.

7. Marc Slonim, *Soviet Russian Literature* (New York: Oxford University Press, 1964), p. 171.

8. At the time the workers were paid "in kind."

9. From Gladkov's diary. Cited in Ul'rikh, p. 48.

10. Kataev cites here Stalin's speech delivered at the First Conference of Industrial Managers in February, 1931.

11. In the *Pedagogical Poem* Makarenko alludes to a newspaper article that referred to him as the "smith of New Men," p. 362.

Chapter 8
THE IRONY OF THE DEED: OLESHA AND PIL'NIAK

1. Trotsky, by that time, had been expelled from the Party and declared an "enemy of the people."

2. According to Luke (4:1-12), floating over the Kidron Valley to astound men by displaying his supernatural powers was the second temptation of Christ. See Ronald Brownrigg, *The New Testament*, vol. 2 of *Who's Who in the Bible* (New York: Bonanza Books, 1980), p. 172.

3. The translation suggested in the novel, "an outcast," I believe, conceals and distorts the meaning with which Pil'niak endowed his characters, "the holy fools." The literal meaning is "a fool and a loafer," see S. I. Ozhegov, editor, *Slovar' Russkogo Iazyka* (Moscow: Izd-vo Sovetskaia Entsiklopediia, 1972).

4. It was during War Communism (1918-1921) that Lenin enunciated his vision of Communist work.

Bibliography

Alexandrova, V. *A History of Soviet Literature,* translated by Mirra Ginsburg. New York: Doubleday & Company, 1963.

Amin, S. *Unequal Development: An Essay on the Social Formations of Peripheral Capitalism.* New York: Monthly Review Press, 1976.

Andreev, L. "K Zvedam. (To the Stars)." In *P'esy.* Moskva: Izd-vo Iskusstvo, 1959.

Arendt, H. *The Human Condition.* Garden City, NY: Doubleday Anchor Books, 1959.

Askol'dov, S. "The Religious Meaning of the Russian Revolution." In *Out of the Depths: A Collection of Articles on the Russian Revolution,* translated and edited by W. F. Woehrlin. Irvine, CA: Schlacks, Jr., 1986.

Behrends, A. J. F. *Socialism and Christianity.* New York: Baker and Taylor, 1886.

Berdyayev, N. "Philosophical Verity and Intelligentsia Truth." In *Signposts,* translated and edited by M. S. Schatz and J. E. Zimmerman. Irvine, CA: Charles Schlacks, Jr., 1986.

_____ . "Russkaia Religioznaia Ideia." In *Problemy Russkogo Religioznogo Soznaniia.* Berlin: YMCA Press, 1923.

_____ . "Specters of the Russian Revolution." In *Out of the Depths: A Collection of Articles on the Russian Revolution,* translated and edited by W. F. Woehrlin. Irvine, CA: Charles Schlacks, Jr., 1986.

Berliner, J. *Factory and Manager in the USSR.* Cambridge: Harvard University Press, 1957.

Bird, A. *A History of Russian Painting.* Boston: G. K. Hall & Co., 1987.

Bonch-Bruevich. V. D. "Sredi Sektantov." *Zhizn'* 6 (1902): 250-270.

Brownrigg, R. "Who's Who in the New Testament. " In *Who's Who in the Bible,* vol. 2. New York: Bonanza Books, 1980.

Bukharin, N. "Speech at the Fifth Komsomol Congress, Oct. 11, 1922." In *Bolsheviks Visions: First Phase of the Cultural Revolution in Soviet Russia,* edited by William G. Rosenberg. Ann Arbor Paperbacks: The University of Michigan Press, 1990.

Bulgakov, S. *Capitalism and Agriculture.* Moscow: n.p., 1901.

_____ . "Heroism and Asceticism (Reflections on the Religious Nature of the Russian Intelligentsia)." In *Signposts,* edited and translated by M. S. Schatz and J. E. Zimmerman. Irvine, CA: Charles Schlacks, Jr., 1986.

Bunin, I. "Derevnia." In *Sobranie Sochinenii.* Berlin: Petropolis, 1934.

Chekhov, A. "Palata No 6 (Ward No. 6)." In Rasskazy, St. Petersburg: A. F. Marks, 1900.

Christian, R. F. *Tolstoy: A Critical Introduction.* Cambridge: Cambridge University Press, 1969.

Crankshaw, E. *The Shadows of the Winter Palace.* New York: Viking, 1976.

Dal', V. I. *Tolkovyi Slovar' Novogo Velikorusskogo Iazyka.* 3rd ed., edited by Baudouin de Courtenay. St. Petersburg: M. O. Wolf, 1909.

_____ . *Poslovitsy i Pogovorki Russkogo Naroda.* Tom I and II. Moscow: Khud. Lit-ra, 1984.

_____ . *Tolkovyi Slovar' Zhivogo Velikorusskogo Iazyka.* 7th ed. Moscow: Russkii Iazyk, 1978.

Eastman, M. "Humiliation of Boris Pil'niak." In *Artists in Uniform: A Study of Literature and Bureaucratism.* New York: Alfred A. Knopf, 1934.

"Evoliutsiia Latyshskogo Krestianstva." *Zhizn'* 6 (1902): 287-306.

Fedotov, G. P. *The Russian Religious Mind.* vol. 2. Cambridge: Harvard University Press, 1946.

Frank, A. G. *Capitalism and Underdevelopment in Latin America: Historical Studies of Chile and Brazil.* New York: Monthly Review Press, 1969.

_____ . "The Development of Underdevelopment." *Political Economy of Development and Underdevelopment,* edited by Ch. K. Wilber. New York: Random House Business Division, 1988.

Geertz, C. *The Interpretation of Culture.* New York: Basic Books, 1973.

_____ . *Local Knowledge.* New York: Basic Books, 1983.

Giddens, A. "Action, Subjectivity and Meaning." In *Aims of Representatation,* edited by M. Krieger. New York: Cambridge University Press, 1987.

_____ . *Capitalism and Modern Social Theory: An Analysis of the Writings of Marx, Durkheim and Max Weber.* Cambridge: Cambridge University Press, 1971.

Gilles, D. *Chekhov: Observer without Illusions,* translated by C. L. Markmann. New York: Funk & Wagnalls, 1968.

Gladkov, F. *Tsement. (Cement).* Moscow: Gos. Izd. Khud. Lit-ra, 1931.

Gomberg-Verzhbinskaia, E. et al., eds. *Vrubel': Perepiska i Vospominania o Khudozhnike.* Leningrad: Iskusstvo, 1976.

Gorky, A. "Mat' (Mother)." In *Sobranie Sochinenii*. vol. 4. Moscow: Gos. Izd-vo Khud. Lit-ra, 1960.

Greenblatt, S. J. *Learning to Curse*. New York: Routledge, 1990.

Joyce, P., ed. *The Historical Meaning of Work*. Cambridge: Cambridge University Press, 1987.

Kagarlitsky, B. *The Thinking Reed*, translated by B. Pearce. London: Verso, 1988.

Kaplanova, S. *Vrubel'*. Leningrad: Avrora Art Publishers, 1975.

Kataev, V. "Vremia, Vpered! (Time, Forward!)" In *Sobranie Sochinenii*. vol. I. Moscow: Gos. Izd-vo Khud. Lit-ra, 1956.

Kautsky, K. "The Commonwealth of the Future." *Essential Works of Socialism*, edited by I. Howe. New Haven: Yale University Press, 1976.

Kemp-Welch, A. *Stalin and the Literary Intelligentsia, 1928-1938*. New York: St. Martin Press's, 1991,

Korolenko, V. G. "S Dvukh Storon." In *Sobranie Sochinenii*, vol. III. Moscow: Izd-vo Pravda, 1971.

Kryzytsky, S. *The Works of Ivan Bunin*. The Hague: Mouton, 1971.

Leites, N. *Soviet Style in Management*. New York: Crane & Russak, 1985.

Lenin, V. "Chto Delat'?" *Sobranie Sochinenii*. 5th edition. Moscow: Izd-vo Polit. Lit-ra, 1960.

_____ . "From the Destruction of the Ancient Social System to the Creation of the New." In *Selected Works IX*. New York: International Publishers, 1937.

_____ . "A Great Beginning." In *Selected Works IX*. New York: International Publishers, 1937.

_____ . "Letters 1920-1923." In *Collected Works 45*. London: Lawrence and Wishart, 1970.

_____ . "The New Economic Policy and the Tasks of the Political Education Department." In *Selected Works IX.* New York: International al Publishers, 1937.

_____ . *The State and Revolution.* Moscow: n.p., n.d.

Lewin, M. *The Making of the Soviet System.* New York: Pantheon Books, 1985.

Lewis, R. W. B. *The American Adam.* Chicago: The University of Chicago Press, 1955.

Loomis, C. and Rytina, J. *Marxist Theory and Indian Communism: A Sociologial Interpretation.* Ann Arbor: Michigan State University Press, 1970.

Makarenko, A. *Pedagogicheskaia Poema (The Pedagogical Poem).* Moscow: Gos. Izd-vo Khud. Lit-ra, 1952.

McClelland. "Business Drive and National Achievement." In *Social Change*, edited by A. and E. Etzioni. New York: Basic Books, 1964.

Nove, A. *The Soviet Economic System.* 3d ed. Boston: Allen and Unwin, 1986.

Olesha, Iu. "Speech at the First All-Union Congress of Writers" (1934). In *Zavist': Izbrannoe.* Michigan, Pullman: Russian Language Specialties, 1973.

_____ . *Zavist': Izbrannoe.* Michigan, Pullman: Russian Language Specialties, 1973.

Ozhegov, S. editor. *Slovar' Russkogo Iazyka.* Moscow: Izd-vo Sovetskaia Entsiklopediia, 1972.

Parsons, T. "Characteristics of Industrial Societies." In *The Transformation of Russian Society,* edited by C. Black. Cambridge: Harvard University Press, 1960.

Pil'niak, B. "Mahogany." In *A Bilingual Collection of Russian Short*

Stories II, edited and translated by M. Friedberg and R. A. Maguire. New York: Random House, 1965.

Propp, V. *Theory and History of Folklore*, edited by A. Liberman. Minneapolis: University of Minnesota Press, 1984.

Prugavin, A. S. "Sredi Sektantov." *Zhizn'* 6 (1902): 258-272.

_____ . *O L've Tolstom i Tolstovstsakh (Concerning Leo Tolstoy and His Disciples)*. Moskva: n. p., 1911.

_____ . *Raskol i Sektantstvo v Russkoi Narodnoi Zhizni*. Moscow: n. p., 1905.

_____ . *Raskol Vverkhu*. Sant-Petrburg: n. p., 1909.

Rigby, T. N. *Stalin*. Englewood Cliffs NJ: Prentice-Hall, 1966.

Roeder, P. G. *Soviet Political Dunamics*. New York: Harper and Row, 1988.

Ruccio, D. F. and Simon, L. H. "Radical Theories of Development: Frank, the Modes of Production School, and Amin." In *The Political Economy of Development and Underdevelopment*, edited by C. K. Wilber. New York: Random House Business Division, 1988.

Russel, R. *Valentin Katyaev*. Boston: Twayne Publishers, 1981.

Schatz, M. S., and J. E. Zimmerman, eds. and trans. "Introduction." In *Signposts: A Collection of Articles on the Russian Intelligentsia*. Irvine, CA: Charles Schlacks, Jr. 1986.

Schlapentokh, V. "Attitudes and Behavior of Soviet Youth in the 1970s and 1980s: The Mysterious Variable in Soviet Politics." In *Research in Political Sociology*. vol. 2. Greenwich, CT: JAI Press, 1986.

Simmons, E. J. *Leo Tolstoy*. Boston: Little, Brown and Company, 1946.

Slonim, M. *Soviet Russian Literature*. New York: Oxford University Press, 1964.

Smelser, N. J. "Toward a Theory of Modernization." In *Social Change,* edited by A. and E. Etzioni. New York: Basic Books, 1967.

Smirnov, A. M, editor. "Sbornik Velikorusskikh Skazok. " *Zapiski Russkogo Geograficheskogo Obshchestva.* XLIV, vol.1, 2. Petrograd: Rossiiskaia Akademiia Nauk, 1917.

So, A. Y. *Social Change and Development: Modernization, Dependency, and World-System Theories.* Newbury Park, CA: Sage Publications, 1990.

Spence, G. W. *Tolstoy the Acetic.* New York: Barnes and Noble, 1968.

Stalin, J. "Foundations of Leninism." In *Stalin's Kampf,* edited by M. R. Werner, New York: Howell, Soskin and Co., 1940.

_____ . "Speech at the First All-Union Conference of Managers of Soviet Industry. February 4, 1931." In *Stalin's Kampf,* edited by M. R. Werner. New York: Howell, Soskin and Co., 1940.

Terras, V. *A History of Russian Literature.* New Haven: Yale University Press, 1991.

Tolstoy, L. N. "Dnevniki." *Sobranie Sochinenii.* vols. 19 and 20 Moscow: Izd-vo Khud. Lit-ra,1965.

_____ . "Confession." In *Polnoe Sobranie Sochinenii,* edited by V. G. Chertkov et al. vol. LXII. Moscow: n.p., 1928-1958.

_____ . "Ne Delanie." *Sochineninia Grafa L. N. Tolstogo (Collected Works of Count L. N. Tolstoy).* Part 14, 10th ed. Moscow: Tovarishch. I. N. Kushnerev i Ko, 1897.

Ul'rikh, L. N. *Letopos' Zhizni i Tvorchestva Gladkova.* Tashkent: Fan, 1982.

Wallerstein, I. *The Modern World-System I.* San Diego: CA: Academic Press, 1974.

Weber, Max. *The Protestant Ethic and the Spirit of Capitalism.* New York: Free Press, 1958.

Weil, I. *Gorky.* New York: Random House, 1966.

Wilson, *A. N. Tolstoy*. New York: W. W. Norton and Company, 1988.

Wolfe, B. D. *Three Who Made a Revolution: A Bibliographical History*. New York: The Dial Press, 1964.

Yanowitch, M. *Work in the Soviet Union: Attitudes and Issues*. New York: M.E. Sharpe, Inc., 1985.

Zenkovsky, V. V. *Russkie Mysliteli i Evropa*. Paris: YMCA Press n. d.

_____ . *A History of Russian Philisophy,* translated by George L. Kline. 2 vols. New York: Columbia University Press, 1953.

Zile, Z., ed. *Ideas and Forces in Soviet Legal History*. New York: Oxford University Press, 1992.

Index

Achievement, value of, 10
Activity, human, 15, 125; core values of, 132; marginal, 125; Russian meaning of, 132
Alexandrova, Vera, 115
Alienation, 5
Ambition, personal: collective and, 122; misery of, 59; pursuit of 17; Russian meaning of work and, 136
Amin, Samir, 11
Andreev, Leonid: Christ the activist and 135; Gorky and, 67, 68; heroic deed, conception of, 68; intellectual endeavor, conception of, 69-70; *K Zvezdam (To the Stars)*, 67-71; Kataev and, 99, 106; Makarenko and, 113; passion of Christ, 70; social change, 73; Tolstoy and, 101
Aphorisms, 28
Aquinas, Thomas, 6
Arendt, Hanna, 4, 5, 6
Artistic expression, 14

Ascetic life, 66
Asceticism, 43, 44
Askol'dov, Sergei, 15

Behrends, A. J. F., 84, 87
Berdyayev, Nikolai: sobornost' (collectivity), 2; Bulgakov and, 17, 35,37; freedom, personal, 45, 48; freedom, philosophy of, 47-48; freedom of will, 46; labor, spiritual, 48; liberation, political, 46; Marxism and, 45, 46; redemption, source of, 47; and revolutionary intelligentsia, 46; social change, 46-47; Tolstoy, criticism of, 47-48; utilitarianism, criticism of, 47
Biblical images, Christian, 15
Bolshevik ideology of labor, 8
Bolshevik leaders: heroic martyrs, 7; Marxism, 7; work ethic, vision of, 3, 14, 18, 83, 123

About the Author

ANNA FELDMAN LEIBOVICH was born and raised in the former Soviet Union. She has worked as a teacher and as a translator in the United States, Israel, and the former Soviet Union. She is currently codirector of the Intercultural Studies Project in the Multinational Institute of American Studies at New York University.